for Gillian

Design and production by
Stephen Troussé at The Poetry Society

Illustrations by
Anna-Louise Barclay at MONSTER

CONTENTS

PREFACE

IN OCTOBER 1997 The Poetry Society held a party to celebrate National Poetry Day, and decided to invite those teachers who had promoted poetry actively in their schools over the previous year. We contacted The Arvon Foundation to find out which schools had taken groups on courses, we looked at the winning entries to the major poetry competitions, we invited those who had been awarded grants or employed poets regularly and we looked up the addresses of all the teachers whose pupils had won the *The Times Educational Supplement* 'Young Poet of the Week'. One name kept re-appearing: Cliff Yates. The poet-selectors for Young Poet of the Week seemed to have spotted this recurrence as well, remarking on several occasions that the poem they had chosen came from 'an excellent group of poems' or 'another excellent set of work'. Clearly this was not a one-off small group of children in an after-school club, or a voluntary group of some kind. Nor was the work the result of a poet's visit or annual festival - children throughout the school were writing poetry all year, and the standard was remarkably high.

Shortly afterwards, *The Times Educational Supplement* sent the poet Kate Clanchy to Maharishi School to report on the secret of their success. Creative writing was clearly valued in the school, and success in poetry or story-writing was as much a matter of pride for staff and pupils as achievement in sport or examination results. Poetry was visible in the school, published work as well as that written in-house. Maybe the secret was rooted in the school's teaching of Transcendental Meditation? But it seemed Cliff's pupils from previous schools had been similarly successful in poetry without the benefit of TM. Maybe it was because he himself is a writer? But there are several poets working as teachers, teachers who write, and schools with poets-in-residence. What was happening at Maharishi School that was not happening anywhere else, and how could it best be passed on to other practitioners?

It's only now I have read *Jumpstart* that I begin to see how poetry really can come to life in a secondary school, and to appreciate how Cliff's subtle modification of life in an ordinary English classroom can bring literature within the grasp of a great many more young people. The central tenet of the *Jumpstart* philosophy is simple enough – that reading and writing poetry are interconnected activities. For young people to approach writing poetry with confidence and ambition they not only have to be familiar with a range of poetry, but also to be in the habit of seeing texts 'from the inside', that is, as writers.

Jumpstart is peppered with suggestions of 'Things to do with a Poem' which range from the simplest, learning it by heart, (including methods of learning by heart as a group activity) and copying it out (yes, that's what writers do, a lot of them, and, yes, it has as much to do with writing as reading), to predicting its contents from the title down, stanza by stanza. The two things that strike me about all of these, is that they are closely related to the 'natural' or spontaneous reaction to verse, and that they are things I was never asked or expected to do in school. Although I was familiar with poetry-reading habits, and had observed on many occasions how reading and hearing poetry leads almost universally to an attempt on writing, I had always assumed that the practice of reading poetry was something incompatible with secondary school life. After all, non-linear texts, or those that require re-visiting are not best adapted to class work, any more than poetry-writing practices which again rely on barely-describable processes of distraction, diversion, re-visiting and revision.

The combination of a dense formal structure and an unpredictable set of responses make even the best-versed teachers shy of bringing poetry into school unless it either makes the students laugh, or is connected to their studies by subject matter rather than by form.

Most of the activities in *Jumpstart* are adapted from adult poetry workshop structures: I'm not sure which is the more surprising – the fact that these are not universally used in schools, or the fact that it is possible at all. Cliff Yates cites his most significant formative moments as a teacher as those in 'workshop' situations – those he attended as part of the Cheshire Poetry Project that led to his own first 'real' poems, those where he felt for the first time the terror of reading back, those where he first realised that this really was possible in a classroom, not just as a break from routine, but as a central part of his teaching of literature and language. Although this book can tell you how workshopping can change your classroom, it cannot replace the experience of trying one for yourself.

If poetry is a craft, and therefore one that must be learned from those practising it, then how can we do this without all turning into poets, or employing poets to sit around in every classroom? This is the book to reassure you that neither of those is necessary, because at its heart is the notion that poetry is teachable, and that everyone can get better at it, and that includes the teachers. This is not a fool-proof set of crib-sheets or short-cuts – having read it, you will realise that a good poem is the only 'how to' manual you need. As well as giving you the confidence to see poems as both your starting point and your set of instructions, *Jumpstart* contains a range of modern poetry that has been tried and tested with young people, as well as a selection of their responses. It is unique in bringing together work for and by young people, and in showing how the gap between the two can be bridged.

SIÂN HUGHES

EDUCATION DEVELOPMENT OFFICER, THE POETRY SOCIETY

INTRODUCTION

WRITING POEMS IN the classroom is unlike anything else. Poems are both liberating and challenging. They are liberating for the less able and the most able pupil. Poems are free from the constraints of prose so that the writer doesn't have to worry about writing in sentences or using 'correct' punctuation. Poems are challenging because of the demands of form and the discipline of saying a great deal in a few lines. At the same time they provide an opportunity to take risks with language and experiment. Writing poems has a refreshing, unpredictable quality, so that the most disaffected pupils can surprise themselves by what they write.

Writing a story is a marathon for some pupils, whereas the first draft of a poem can be a ten minute sprint. Poems are mostly short, which makes redrafting more acceptable; even if pupils think they have 'finished' a poem, you can always ask them to write an extra draft for a class anthology or display. Every word counts, so that drafting poems provides an opportunity to teach pupils about language in a context that is important to them. The skills learnt in writing poems improves pupils' writing in all other areas, and improves their awareness of language in anything that they subsequently read. Finally, with poems we are onto a winner; pupils spontaneously memorise poems of varying quality (in the form of song lyrics) for pleasure, and many will write poems anyway, at some time or other, for themselves.

For these reasons, and probably for others as well, lessons on writing poems are, for me, the best part of teaching English. I came into teaching late. I left school as soon as I could for the printing factory, and, after a variety of jobs, studied for 'A' levels at the local FE college, then worked my way through a couple of degrees. I have been teaching English for nineteen years. I taught throughout the age and ability range at 3 different comprehensive schools in Cheshire where I was also a member of the Cheshire Poetry Project. I am Deputy Head and English teacher at Maharishi School in Skelmersdale where pupils and teachers practise Transcendental Meditation and where the development of the students' creative potential is a priority. I am also Poetry Society Poet in Residence for Secondary Education. I run workshops for young people in schools and colleges, workshops for adults, and INSET courses on poetry.

When I started teaching I was uneasy about showing pupils how to write poems. (I don't think you can 'teach' anyone how to write; the best you can do is show them, they learn it for themselves.) This unease is shared by many English teachers I speak to. It was like trying to show students how to draw and paint, armed only with qualifications in Art History. University had prepared me to criticise and theorise, not how to write or understand the process of writing. There's a world of difference between responding to a poem in a university seminar and responding to a poem written by a pupil in Year 8.

I decided that the way into the business of writing poems was to talk with writers. The opportunity came with the Cheshire Poetry Project, set up to devise materials for teaching poetry in Cheshire schools and colleges. The philosophy was sound; give a group of teachers the time and resources, and they will devise practical, effective teaching materials. The key to the project was the opportunity to work alongside writers.

Around this time, inspired by working on the project, I started to write poems. Ian McMillan came into our school and things were never quite the same again. He introduced me to poetry magazines (in which my poems started to appear), encouraged me to go on an Arvon Foundation course at Lumb Bank, and opened my eyes to some of the things that are possible in the classroom. I also began to attend writing workshops.

The experience of writing workshops was invaluable; it was the first time that I had ever written in that kind of environment. It was both relaxed and pressured, friendly and disciplined; it fitted exactly, therefore, with the classroom atmosphere which I had learned how to establish. There were elements of the workshop that lent themselves ideally to the classroom; the rapid changes in pace, the different kinds of preparation for writing, the actual intensity of the writing itself, and reading back. The only experience I had previously had of writing in a group was when I was at school. There was no comparison. I knew immediately that this would influence the way I taught writing, and set about adapting the workshop approach to the classroom.

The writing workshop is also based on mutual respect; no one can write in a group which doesn't take this for granted, just as no pupil will do their best if they think that what they say or write is not valued. We know as English teachers that the most fundamental ingredient in all successful teaching, including the teaching of poetry, is this relationship of trust between teacher and pupil. It is an instinctive thing; if pupils know that you are really listening to them, they will talk about what they consider important. And the same applies to writing.

Attending workshops and writing poems radically altered the way I responded to students' poems. As Peter Sansom says in the interview in Chapter 9:

> The difference is not looking at the poem from the outside, like a finished artefact, but from the inside. It's a living thing, not part of the canon of English literature.

Reading and writing poems became related activities, not only for me personally, but also in the classroom. To write poems, pupils need to read them. Poems themselves, of course, can also be valuable models for students' own writing. It is also true that writing poems helps give young people the confidence and insight to be able to read well. Both activities inform each other. When I set out to write this book, it was going to be about writing poems, not reading them; I soon discovered that I had to deal with both; I couldn't write about one without the other. So this book works in two ways; it describes how I get pupils to write poems and it also describes some of the ways in which I approach the reading of poems in the classroom. I haven't attempted to deal with all aspects of teaching poetry but have concentrated on those areas that I find most useful when it comes to getting young people to write poems.

The poems I have used here are mostly contemporary. It is also possible to use pre-twentieth century poetry as a stimulus for writing, but contemporary poems are more useful in this context because they are mostly closer in style to how young people actually speak. It's important to challenge the assumption that poetry has to sound 'poetic', which usually means that it should sound like Keats, for example, or Tennyson. As Peter Sansom says, in *Writing Poetry*, talking about 'On First Looking Into Chapman's Homer':

> Keats's 'true voice of feeling', the honesty, fluency and depth of his imagination, these are timeless. The way it is expressed, though, is tied to the time he wrote. The syntax and diction which place the poem in Keats's time equally take it out of ours.

Young people need to learn to write in their own voice, and in order to find their own voice they need to listen to the voices of their contemporaries. As Ted Hughes argues in *Poetry in the Making*: 'Reading Milton or Keats to children is one thing. Asking them, or allowing them, to use such as models for their own writing is another'. He talks about the dangers of striving for 'a stylistic ideal' when teaching pupils to write, and believed that teachers, should have nothing to do with this:

> Their words should be not "How to write" but "How to try to say what you really mean" – which is part of the search for self-knowledge and perhaps, in one form or another, grace.

All the ideas and approaches described in this book are for this; to enable young people to say what they really mean. Not what they think they ought to say, not to please us, but to please themselves.

CLIFF YATES
SKELMERSDALE, MAY 1999

1::HENRY'S CLOCK

I WANT PUPILS to get into the habit of writing poems. I give them an exercise book for notes, drafts and poems. I don't mark it; this is for their eyes only, and it can be untidy (if they're drafting, it should be untidy). I encourage them to record anything that might come in handy for poems: fragments of overheard conversation, words they like the sound of, unusual things that happen to them. The notebook is a way of allowing pupils to work as writers, to see writing poems as a normal, everyday activity, as valid as keeping a diary, making notes or writing letters.

If during a lesson there is time to spare, I give a class the option of writing a poem in their books, and many do. Some will write poems at home, not because it's 'homework', but simply because they want to; they will have a backlog of first and second drafts, which they will return to, a series of poems that they are working on.

Whenever I can, I write with the class. When it comes to reading back, I'll sometimes do that too. What I write won't necessarily be that good, but that's not important; writing is about taking chances and trying things out, we don't always have to turn out something we're satisfied with. Sometimes the pupils see the whole process, with my own poems, from first draft to final publication...

It's first thing Monday morning, Year 9. Henry is talking about his new alarm clock. I write something in my notebook. Some poems you can spend ages on, some arrive almost complete, like this one. I just need the ending. A day or two later the last stanza arrives, and I send the poem off to Alan Ross at *London Magazine*. It's accepted, and published a few weeks later. I take in the magazine and read out the poem:

HENRY'S CLOCK

Henry's alarm stops ringing when you shout.
He likes to set it for one minute
and shout 'STOP!' It is satisfying

but not intelligent. If you shout,
'CARRY ON!' it stops. It does not discriminate
between happiness, anger and despair.

If you like, you can shout,
'THE RIDERS ARE TRAMPLING THE NIGHT
ON THEIR TERRIBLE SHINING HORSES!'

Henry grins. This kind of thing doesn't happen all the time, obviously – but it's great when it does. The principle is that poetry is attainable. It isn't something 'out there', belonging to an elite, it's part of everyday life.

A week or so later, Luke comes into the classroom thirsty after playing football. 'Dehydrated', he says. He likes the sound of it, says it again. 'Dehydrated – in the English room'. He gets his exercise book and writes:

DEHYDRATED IN THE ENGLISH ROOM

Parched with thirst
We loll on our desks
Trying to drink
Bottles of Quink.

We cannot pay attention to the English teacher;
Too busy licking lips,
Feeling sick,
Stomachs contracting.

The girls are licking the condensation off the windows
But there isn't much left; the first years have already been at it.
Someone has a chemical from the lab
And it looks like water . . .

Children wasted on the floor, some sucking rubbers cross-eyed,
Cheeks sucked in like goldfish.
Ink bottles empty, children wither in their seats
And the English teacher still hasn't noticed.

Luke (Year 9)

Sometimes a pupil will get a poem published, or win a competition. I tell them that 'winning' isn't the most important thing, and I'm serious. But as long as we bear this in mind, and not take them too seriously, some competitions can directly benefit our pupils. Good competitions are of value because they provide an audience for pupils' work and a chance to get published. They also provide a handy incentive to take drafting another stage further.

Competitions

Some teachers are wary of competitions, and for good reason. I only enter pupils' work for ones that I am sure about. They have to follow these requirements:

1 Pupils should not have to pay to enter.

2 If their poem is successful they should receive at least a free copy of the book in which it is to be published.

3 The judges, ideally, should be poets. If the judges know nothing about poetry, the results will have little meaning.

4 Pupils should not lose copyright unless they are fully aware of what this entails, and if the competition is for a good cause (like the Roald Dahl Foundation Poetry Competition) or winning the competition is so good for the writer that it's possibly worth it (like W. H. Smith Young Writers).

If you are unsure about a competition or opportunity for young writers, contact the Poetry Society who will tell you what I am going to say now: avoid vanity publishers at all costs!

In fact the best way of getting pupils' poems published is not a competition, in the strict sense, at all. It is the *Times Educational Supplement* 'Young Poet of the Week' column, where a well-known guest poet selects and comments on the poems. Long may it continue.

When I get the pupils writing poems, the last thing on my mind is competitions. What I am after is for the writers to engage in language and be able to express what they want through poems. One of the ways in which they learn how to do this is by using poems as models. This approach liberates the pupil from making decisions about form and approach. If you choose the poems carefully, the experience can have a direct benefit on all their subsequent writing. This is especially true with pupils who are not used to writing poems in this way, who might have a rigid idea of what a poem is or should be. Just the experience of reading certain poems and using them as models can provide a real breakthrough in their writing.

The most exciting poems to read with a class, the ones that lead to the big breakthroughs, are often deceptively simple, like this one:

THIS IS JUST TO SAY

I have eaten
the plums
that were in
the icebox

and which
you were probably
saving
for breakfast

Forgive me
they were delicious
so sweet
and so cold

William Carlos Williams

This is one of my favourite poems, in terms of its impact in the classroom. It challenges preconceptions about poetry, and this is always useful.

After reading William Carlos Williams with Year 8 recently, I took the class outside with exercise books and got them to take 'poem-photos' of whatever they saw; to take their time and lay the words out on the page as deliberately as Williams does. Williams spent hours re-typing his poems late at night, after coming in from work, so the simplicity hides complete dedication to the craft of writing.

The way to read Williams is slowly. I remember getting the two hefty volumes of the *Collected Poems* out of Swansea University library and taking them into Singleton Park, on a bench. After twenty minutes I knew for certain that Williams would not have appreciated such huge volumes for his poems; it's a bit like a suitcase full of chocolates.

I sometimes introduce 'This is Just to Say' by talking about Williams, who spent his working life as a doctor, writing in his spare time. I tell pupils how he came back late one night after treating a patient, found the plums in the fridge, ate them and left the note for this wife. Sometimes I write the poem out in prose and don't tell them it is a poem. Then get them to put it into lines and stanzas, at some stage suggesting four line stanzas. This is useful for talking about line and stanza breaks, which is very useful for their own writing.

The shape of the poem is also worth exploring: what would a doctor write on, most of the time? The back of a prescription pad. What difference does it make writing on different size paper? Give them massive sheets of paper and small pieces, for writing on. See what difference it makes.

Is Williams really and truly sorry for eating the plums? How can you tell? Have the children ever apologised for something they have done that they enjoyed doing? What? You can get some good oral work out of this, and some cracking poems. I've had all types; smashed vases, ink on furniture, an apology made by aliens from the safety of their spaceship after destroying Earth. You can use this with any age group including sixth formers, where it's particularly useful to prompt a discussion on what is poetry.

What is poetry?

I suspect there are as many definitions of poetry as there are poets. What matters is the question, and it's a fruitful one. If we have challenging anthologies in the classroom, pupils' notion of poetry and their view of what is possible will benefit tremendously. What makes the following a poem?

8.06 p.m. June 10th 1970

poem

Tom Raworth

At University I was taught that each word in a poem should earn its place. How far is this true of Tom Raworth's poem? What difference does it make if we change the title to '8.07 p.m. June 10th 1970'? Did something happen on that date? Is he playing games with our notion of what a poem is? Write this poem on the board (or pass around copies of the anthology *Against the Grain*, in which it appears) and ask them to tell you about it. Guaranteed to provoke.

Tom Raworth writes:

> The poem is one of a sequence, *STAG SKULL MOUNTED*. It simply reflects a period when I started with the conceit of thinking I would graph those moments when a poem arrives... hence the precision of the times and dates. I thought I'd work out whether there was a graph or something... but then that became boring. So finally they [the dates] just became the titles of the poems... because the poems are in some way the explanations and contradictions of those particular moments. So... at that time, [8.06 p.m. June 10th 1970] the word 'poem' prodded me to write it. So I did, and checked in the dictionary I had then beside me, and found that 'poem' by itself satisfied EVERY definition in there of a poem, except the proviso that 'some poems may rhyme': so obviously the next one, a minute or so later, was
>
> poem
> poem

Another poem that challenges the reader's assumptions about what makes a poem a poem is this:

SONNY BOY WILLIAMSON IS TRYING TO COOK A RABBIT IN A KETTLE

Ingredients:

1. Rabbit
2. Water

Method:

1. Attempt to get lid off kettle.
2. Attempt to get lid off kettle.
3. Attempt to put rabbit in kettle.

4. Use harmonica to squeeze rabbit in kettle.
5. Switch kettle on.
6. Settle down to watch *My Friend Flicka* on huge black and white 1960s hotel TV.
7. Inspect kettle. Trouser press switched on by mistake.
8. Take toast out of trouser press and eat it. Tastes of trousers.
9. Switch kettle on.
10. Settle down to watch *My Mother The Car* on huge black and white 1960s hotel TV.
11. Smell burning.
12. Hit top of TV with harmonica.
13. Smell burning.
14. Attempt to put burning kettle out with small plastic 1960s containers of hotel milk.
15. Run from the room shouting I TRIED TO COOK A RABBIT IN A KETTLE BUT THE KETTLE CAUGHT FIRE.
16. Realise that's a catchy tune.
17. Sing it: I TRIED TO COOK A RABBIT IN A KETTLE BUT THE KETTLE CAUGHT FIRE . . .

Ian McMillan

The essence of a recipe is that it should be the same every time; Ian McMillan confounds the reader's expectations of the form by using it to write about something unrepeatable, the 'apocryphal tale' of Sonny Boy Williamson. Apart from confounding expectations of what a poem is (always a useful thing to do with a class) the poem is a useful model. Ask the class to write their own recipe poem in which they describe something that happened that could probably never be repeated.

'Sonny Boy Williamson Is Trying To Cook A Rabbit In A Kettle' is hugely entertaining; it is a poem I look forward to reading with a class. So is the next poem.

THE UNCERTAINTY OF THE POET

I am a poet.
I am very fond of bananas.

I am bananas.
I am very fond of a poet.

I am a poet of bananas.
I am very fond,

A fond poet of 'I am, I am' –
Very bananas,

Fond of 'Am I bananas'
Am I? – a very poet.

Bananas of a poet!
Am I fond? Am I very?

Poet bananas! I am.
I am fond of a 'very'.

I am of very fond bananas.
Am I a poet?

Wendy Cope

This poem was written in response to the strange, dreamlike painting by Giorgio de Chirico, *The Uncertainty of the Poet*. I'm not going to attempt to describe the painting but it does include a steam train, a pile of bananas and the bust of the Venus de Milo. You don't have to know this to enjoy the poem. Any class will respond to this. It's a great poem for reading aloud in groups, trying out a variety of tones and moods.

For a poem of their own, ask them to write down any three words that they like the sound of, preferably not all to do with the same thing. Then ask them to write a poem like Wendy Cope's, where they restrict themselves mainly to those three words using them in different combinations in two-line stanzas. As a follow-up you can also get them to challenge each other to write poems based on any three words. I last did this when I was Writer in Residence at the West Lancs Young Writers Summer School. The group challenged me to include 'fireman,' 'pizza' and 'book' . Try it! I think it's probably easier to choose words that can be used in different contexts, like 'bananas', and also allow them to change the word slightly, ('book' can become 'booked' for example). This is good preparation also for poetic forms that make use of repeated words such as that tricky heavyweight, the sestina.

The great thing about poems like 'This is Just to Say', 'Sonny Boy Williamson Is Trying To Cook A Rabbit In A Kettle' and ' The Uncertainty Of The Poet' is that they are accessible to read and they work well as models for pupils' poems. Using them as models gives the class a huge amount of confidence because everyone will be able to write something.

It is encouraging when everyone in the class writes a poem. It is often believed that only certain people can write poetry. Peter Sansom talks about this belief, and about the special status that poetry has in schools that makes it possible for someone to be considered good at writing poems, even if they are not particularly good at other aspects of English. It is certainly the case that some pupils with a reputation for being not so good at, say, spelling and punctuation, feel at home writing poems.

Exercises like using such as using 'Sonny Boy Williamson Is Trying To Cook A Rabbit In A Kettle' will help make writing poems into an immensely popular aspect of work in English for pupils of all abilities. Apart from the sheer fun of it, there is something very satisfying about poems: you can spend a few minutes on a haiku or you can spend seven years on one. You still have just the three lines.

2::JUMPSTARTING THE POEM

WHAT IS IT about workshops that make them so effective, and what can we learn from them for the classroom?

Mutual respect

A fundamental assumption of writing workshops is that no one is 'judged' by what they write. This is partly down to the acceptance of uncertainty. Everyone writes, and anything can happen; the most experienced writer can write badly and the most inexperienced can write brilliantly. Knowing this helps to remove anxiety, and to encourage an atmosphere of support and mutual respect. No-one needs to worry that their writing will not be good enough. The most important aspect of a poetry lesson in school is this positive atmosphere in which no-one feels threatened. I can't imagine trying to run a poetry lesson after 'telling off' a class; if I was in the position of having to do that, I would have to change the atmosphere completely, or the activity. To help establish the sense of collaboration and mutual respect, I encourage teachers to write with their pupils, even if it's only for a few minutes during the lesson. Seeing their teacher taking writing seriously encourages pupils to value writing, to see it as important.

Space

A workshop provides space in which to write. You know in advance that you are going to write something, whatever its quality. If it does not lead to a poem, it doesn't matter. Tell pupils that even if they do not come up with a poem, they will have a few ideas written down which they might be able to use somewhere else. The session could yield a good first line, or a stanza that fits into a poem that has already been written. Often during writing workshops I end up writing something that I wanted to write anyway; the idea was already there in the back of my mind, an idea or a feeling, like a kind of pressure. The workshop takes the lid off the pressure, and the poem gets written. Jumpstarting the poem.

Write what you want

The best workshops can be those where you get so carried away with writing that you forget the directions you were supposed to be following. I give pupils permission to do the same thing. The only requirement is that they have to write something. The aim of any writing exercise is simply to achieve a first draft, it is not a recipe which is meant to have the same result each time. Further, while pupils are writing their draft, or working on it during the coming week, it may change into a completely different kind of poem. This is fine. I encourage pupils to surprise me, and to surprise themselves. As I said earlier, many poems contain the element of surprise, good poems often surprise the writer when they are being written.

Playfulness

An important point to make about the value of exercises, and particularly writing games, is that whether or not they lead to a poem, they encourage playfulness, and playfulness with language is central to the way in which many writers, not only poets, work. Joining in writing exercises may not always lead to poems, but trying out ideas and playing about with words is a potent tool in the classroom.

Finishing the poem

A workshop will not necessarily yield a complete poem. How long should we give pupils to write a poem? I generally set up an exercise during one lesson and homework for the week will be to 'finish' the poem. During intervening lessons I might replay the game, or repeat a similar exercise for shorter periods, to give the class more opportunities to complete a first draft. During those lessons I also lay aside time for drafting, when they will have the opportunity to read or hear each other's poems. I will also look at their work and make suggestions. Elsewhere in this book I discuss other ways of writing poems, over a longer period, for example by keeping a notebook. There is a place for a variety of ways of writing poems, I think, or at least there should be. The important thing is to enjoy the process of writing and to be excited by it; when this happens, the poems look after themselves.

The workshop

What about the way in which a workshop is structured? What are the elements of the structure that can readily be translated into the classroom?

1 ***Build up*** The pace of writing workshops, like the pace of any lesson, is important. A short period of intense writing comes after a build-up which might involve a variety of changes of activity, for example a

warm-up exercise, a writing game, making notes in response to a series of questions, or reading a poem that is going to be used as a model. Most of this book, of course, describes build-ups, or ways into writing. One thing that works well is to introduce an idea and then leave it for a while. This allows the pupils to work on it, 'in the back of their minds'. For me, the important part of any poem is often 'written' before I put pen to paper, when it is jogging around inside my head while I'm doing something else, like walking to school. Try telling pupils what they are going to write about at the beginning of the lesson. It's surprising how quickly they will settle to write when the time comes.

2 *Concentrated writing* (for a short period). I will discuss this more fully in the next chapter. A time limit does two things: it provides pressure and removes anxiety. It provides pressure because you only have so long to write, and it removes anxiety because no one can be expected to produce anything in a short amount of time. Peter and Ann Sansom discuss the merits of announcing a short time limit, say 10 minutes, and then allowing longer, as a way of removing anxiety. Pupils don't usually notice (if they do they are usually glad of the extra time) and of course it gives them longer to write.

3 *Reading back* If the session has gone well, pupils will automatically want to do this. If pupils are reluctant, I never insist, just as I won't read aloud a pupil's work without permission. It is important that pupils can write exactly what they want, (and obviously use their discretion about whether it's appropriate to read back what they have written).

Drafting

If there is time, I start work on drafting during the 'workshop' session, if not I will start it next time I see the class. During this time of drafting they can show their poems to their neighbours, or to me. I also give them permission to change activity while drafting, for example to read for a few minutes. What often happens is that a change of focus enables pupils to mull over ideas in the back of their minds, and come back to the poem fresh. Drafting is so important that I have sections on it throughout this book. However, there is one important point that is so relevant that I am going to include it here.

Drafting: the first draft

At this stage of the workshop the poems should be regarded strictly as a first draft. There is a tendency, even among some fairly experienced writers, to get attached to a first draft and to be reluctant to change it. I remember this when I started to write; I was so uncertain about whether or not the first draft was 'any good' that I was loathe to change it. The point to make is that however much a poem is changed, the pupil still has the original draft, and can choose keep it in preference to all subsequent drafts. (It does sometimes happen that the first draft is the best.) The best policy with pupils is to give them as much experience of drafting as possible. To overcome the fear of becoming over-attached to a first draft and being unwilling to 'spoil' it, to get pupils used to drafting, I recommend using group poems.

Drafting group poems

I will describe how to write the first draft of specific group poems later on in this chapter. However, the main principle is the same throughout. The procedure I am about to describe assumes that, doing one of the exercises described in this book (such as the bag of words), you are at the stage when you have a lot of notes on the board, which you are about to use for a first draft. You can demonstrate drafting in three different ways.

1 Show the group how you would draft it if it was your poem, by drafting it on the board, talking them through your decisions.

2 Draft it with them, asking them what they want for a first line, for example, and which words or ideas to include or leave out. If there is disagreement you can take a vote. Encourage pupils to go for 'what sounds best' and not to vote for their friend's idea, for example – tell them it is okay to change their minds.

3 Ask everyone in the class, working alone or in groups, to use the first draft for a complete poem of their own. The advantage of working on their own is that the pupils will be happy to change it around because they will not see it as their own poem, therefore it gives them experience of drafting without feeling particularly attached to the words in front of them. You can also get them to compare different versions and discuss

preferences. The advantage of working in groups at this stage is that they will have to talk through and justify their decisions.

The furniture game

I have a fondness for this game because it was while participating in it that I wrote what I considered to be my first 'real' poem. It was on a residential course for Cheshire English teachers at the Menai Centre in Anglesey and the poet Pete Morgan was running the workshop. I'll never forget the actual feeling of writing that poem. It was the first time I had written in this kind of workshop; the atmosphere and focus was something I had not experienced before.

I also remember how nervous I was to read back what I had written; I was almost shaking. I think I learnt more in this brief session than in hours of teacher training, not only how to set up a workshop-type lesson, but also what is involved in asking pupils to read back. For this reason I would encourage all English teachers who haven't already done so, to attend at least one writing workshop, run along these lines. If my experience is anything to go by, the classroom will never be the same again.

Another reason for my fondness for this exercise is that it is guaranteed to work: everyone ends up with a poem. The account I am going to give is developed from the Furniture Game described by Sandy Brownjohn in *Does It Have To Rhyme?*. The furniture game also provides a memorable introduction to metaphor.

This is how it works. Someone thinks of a person known to everyone in the group and the rest of the class have to guess who it is by asking such questions as, 'if this person were a piece of furniture, what would they be?'. Other questions might be what weather/vehicle/landscape/drink/piece of music/building would they be? And so on. The only information that can be revealed about the person is whether they are male or female, alive or dead. You can also have a fiction/non-fiction category.

The person questioned should say the first answer that comes into their heads, and if nothing suggests itself they should 'pass'. The main thing is to make the questions general rather than specific, so that there are more possibilities. For example, 'what article of clothing would they be?' is more useful than 'what colour trousers?' and 'if they were growing in a garden, what would they be?' is more useful than 'what type of weed?' The speed with which they sometimes guess the name of the person illustrates the power of metaphor.

Pupils take it in turns to be asked questions until everyone has a list of images from which poems can be crafted. The first time you do this, write someone's answers on the board and demonstrate how to use them as the first draft of a poem, by rearranging and connecting the images, perhaps into a kind of narrative ('James Bond' by William Kerley, makes use of a narrative structure), or description, using suggestions from the class. This is the most exciting part: the transformation of list into poem.

There are plenty of alternatives when it comes to structuring these poems; the whole poem can be based upon one metaphor, for example: what room? what is in the room? what is the view from the window? etc. Or each stanza can be based upon one image. When the class have written the first draft, tell them it is fine to introduce anything they know of the person, any facts or stories (like Joe Broughton does with 'Swarby', which for this reason is less recognisably a 'furniture poem'); at this stage it is no longer a guessing game, it is a poem.

Organisation

It is time-consuming to have everyone in the class come to the front and be asked questions by the whole class. An alternative is to ask the whole class the same questions at the same time, and get them to write down the answers. Alternatively, put the class into small groups or pairs, and get them to take turns questioning each other. An advantage of using groups is that you can appoint scribes to write down answers, so that if anyone has difficulties with writing, they are not inhibited by this. In groups where the majority have difficulties with writing I would import scribes from a different group, if possible (this works brilliantly, especially if you can get enthusiastic pupils well-trained in writing this type of poem who can help with the process of drafting). Alternatively, I would have everyone come to the front and write down their answers on the board. If time is short, limit the number of questions. Another thing you can do is what Pete Morgan did at the Menai Centre. After playing the game with three or four people coming to the front to ask questions, he simply told us to write our own, trying to base it on one particular metaphor, which we could develop in any way we liked. This works well with more able pupils, Year 10 and older.

PARROT PLUMES

(Furniture poem: John Cleese)

A stick insect man, clothed
In a tinted green tweeded suit, sat
At an antique, shiny handled desk,
Acting out a private school headmaster, his posture
Serious
The situation humorous, music
Of a jazzy classical nature, he dreams
Of being a coal miner, lumberjack or shop keeper
Reminiscing
Of when he was a lad.
A shop full of bizarre animals, colours
Reds, greens, yellows and blues.
A shop full of bright, dead, parrot plumes.

Clare Carline (Year 10)

JAMES BOND

The moveable trolley rockets
Down the privy
Looking for
A restored Aston Martin
Which was looking for
An old stately home.

1964 Fantasy Novel.
Live for the moment;
The glamour, the fame
The thrill
Of when the dining
Room table with 50
Seated guests
Gallahants into
The kitchen.

William Kerley (Year 9)

Drafting: the word processor

The word processor has taken a lot of the hard work out of drafting: the tedium of having to hammer out yet another copy on the typewriter. It is also very good for when a pupil has written something but is loathe to change it. Get them to put it on the word processor, copy it, then play around with the copy, secure in the knowledge that they can always throw it away and go back to the original. Encourage pupils to experiment with form; set the margins really small, for example, to see how the poem looks when it's long and thin. Get them to do crazy things with the shape of their poems on the computer. It's amazing how good ideas turn up when they are simply 'playing'. William Kerley played around with his poem 'James Bond' for ages, experimenting with line breaks, before coming up with his final version. I really like this poem, partly because it is so unpredictable. I'm always suspicious of centring though, because pupils sometimes centre their poems – *all* their poems – because they like the look of it. Centring can distract from the use of line breaks and dilute their power. It's important to explain this to students, then simply leave it up to them. Centring, I know, can be incredibly powerful, like with George Herbert's 'Easter Wings'. Imagine how long it must have taken him to write it out; it would have been so much easier with a word processor. He'd have probably written a whole flock of them.

I was talking earlier about 'jumpstarting' poems: how sometimes you can start writing a poem and end up writing something you hadn't anticipated, the poem that was waiting to be written. The following poem started as a furniture poem. When I taught Joe Broughton he was a great fan of the fiddle player Dave Swarbrick. He'd first seen 'Swarby' play with Fairport Convention at the age of five and was so impressed that as soon as he could he started to learn the fiddle, determined to play as well as Swarby. At the time I taught him English Joe was already performing in gigs.

SWARBY

A fiddle player,
But not just a fiddler.

C sharp with seventy other notes,
In one and a half beats.

The Atholl Highlanders at a hundred miles and hour,
Not how it was wrote!

The Mason's Apron wasn't written in G or C or F sharp minor,
But he manages to change
The key, the notes, the clef, the timing.
The notes, the clef, the timing, the key,
Over and over
Until,
From slow to fast,
From high G to higher G,
He sounds like a high speed dubbing machine!

I've seen him on telly,
I've heard him on tape,
I've played him on video,

Through the smoke.
The smoke that will one day cause his death
Unless the whisky gets him first.

I've seen many a fiddle player,
But since I saw him, nobody
Will have the character,
The wit, the humour,
The speed, the tone,
The tune, the style,
The smile,
The spotty braces of which I have some.

Dave Swarbrick takes a bow!

Joe Broughton (Year 8)

Ten years after writing 'Swarby', Joe Broughton describes how he wrote it:

I was in my bedroom at home where I had just listened to a recording of Dave Swarbrick playing 'The Fiddle Duet' with fellow 'Whippersnapper' band member Chris Leslie and I decided to write a 'furniture poem' about it. First I asked myself questions relating to fiddle playing, but once I hit upon the opening two lines I asked no more questions. The only thing I ever altered from those ten minutes of writing was the title. On Cliff Yates' advice I changed it from 'A Furniture Poem' to 'Swarby'.

I continued playing the fiddle and in my third year at college I landed a job with the Albion Band, run by founder member of Fairport Convention, Ashley Hutchings. A few other funny things have happened. We did a joint gig with Fairport Convention last year when they invited me to the stage to play a number that I had watched Swarby play when I was five. On my 21st birthday I was playing a gig and out of the audience stepped Chris Leslie; we played the fiddle duet that inspired the Swarby poem. Strangely enough, a year or so ago, a seven-year old approached me after a gig and presented me with a poem about myself. That really made me smile...

Bag of words

Cheshire Poetry Project was set up by Michael Jones, Senior English Advisor and co-ordinated by Advisory Teacher John Williams, now Literacy Consultant for Cheshire LEA. The bag of words exercise was developed by John Williams. Here is John's version of the game, from the Cheshire Poetry Pack:

> This is a simple and enjoyable poetry writing technique for all ages and abilities. It encourages children to observe things closely and describe them. It introduces children to the power of metaphor and simile very quickly using their own observations.
>
> The teacher distributes a picture to each member of the class. The Spaceman picture [of an astronaut floating in space] often works best at first. The teacher draws a huge bag on the board and writes at the top 'A BAG OF WORDS'. In the middle of the bag the teacher writes the word 'SPACEMAN' and asks the children to look closely at the picture. The children are asked what the spaceman looks like. It is important that the word 'like' is used. You might have some interesting ideas: a crab, an American footballer; he looks like he has a torch in his hand; his feet are wrapped in cling film; he looks more like a diver; like a baby, and so on. The teacher writes the children's suggestions in the bag until the bag seems 'full'.
>
> Now this is where the magic comes. As an example, the teacher links up the

> words on the board in a poem. You will have to add other words; 'with', 'in', 'nearby', 'he can see', 'above him there is', 'when', and so forth, in order to make clearer links between the phrases. The results can be quite spectacular. When the teacher has finished the example poem on the board, the children can follow the same technique with a new picture. Fascinating results can be achieved using interesting objects: dead leaves, coloured stones, fossils, old maps and so on.

Encourage pupils to be as inventive as possible when you are 'filling the bag', and include all their ideas; they will be surprisingly ruthless when it comes to editing out the weaker ones. Ask them to turn the picture round when they are generating ideas; sideways and upside down – it's surprising how unfamiliar images can appear. Also get them to 'find things' in the picture. I have a massive picture of a crab that looks remarkably like a JCB.

When you are copying out the phrases from the bag, adding prepositions and so on, ask children what line should come next: there will be a surprising amount of agreement. At this stage you can occasionally leave out the word 'like', and demonstrate the change in impact achieved when comparisons are allowed to stand as metaphors. When you have 'finished', focus on the first and last line; ask them to justify their preferences and maybe take a class vote on the final choice.

There is nothing quite like the collaboration involved in writing a class poem, and the sense of achievement when it is completed.

The title does not have to be the source of the poem, you can take a line or image from the 'bag' and use that. This is how Katie arrived at the title of her poem, which was printed in the project pack based upon the picture of the astronaut:

ELECTRIC COWBOY

Behind the spaghetti sky
Echoes the sound of the lasso
Whipping away spiders, snakes and snails.
The fishbowl and sunglass steadily balance
On his shoulders,
Occasionally rocking to the rhythm
Of the radio strapped to his mighty chest.

The battered toothbrush busily cleans
While the connected kettle boils furiously.

Katie (Year 9)

Sometimes the source of the picture can add to the impact of the poem:

OUTLINE OF A VIKING SHIP (AD 1100)

It is a ship of days gone by coming from the mist,
a sail rolled up.
Two lifeboats, one on either side,
one is Concorde coming from the ground,
a nuclear missile,
the other a jet.
It is a cross,
Christ on Calvary hill,
moon of blood,
a man with outstretched hands,
an Indian arrow or a totem pole,
the frame of a wigwam,
a flagpole
or a maypole,
long ribbons carried by ghost children.
There is a weather cock,
a hammer,
a screwdriver,
scales,
a tropical plant.
It is an ancient picture,
a street drawing on a cracked pavement,
a chalk drawing on a blackboard,
hills on a child's picture.

Rachel Head (Year 7)

'Bag of Words' is one way of working with visual images. I tried out a variation on this approach recently, using a picture of a dust mite, magnified thousands of times, that appeared as a double-page spread in the

Times Educational Supplement Friday Magazine's 'Big Picture' (a great resource for poetry lessons). I put the picture up on the board and asked a Year 10 class to write down anything that it made them think of. To add to the impact, I didn't tell them that it was a dust mite. I told them to imagine it incredibly huge, coming across the field at the back of the school. I turned the picture round, to show it from different angles and asked them a series of questions: what noise it would make? what does it reminds you of? what would it be like if it were human? and so on. They had to make notes in reply to these questions. This provides a structure, and sometimes one that they will use in their final poems. I then told them it was a dust mite and gave them some facts and figures which they were free to use in their poems.

AN INVASION

Warning
They have landed.
The disembodied thumbs with legs
Are coming.

We inhale them.
They fill our clothes, pillows, mattresses and carpets,
Stinking and itching.

Less than half a millimetre
Of palm tree and sausage
Feeding on dead skin.

Dermatophagoide,
Dust Mite.

Ben Cross (Year 10)

Structured writing

Structured writing (an account of which I have just described) does not, incidentally, have to be used with visual images. It can also be used it on its own as a writing exercise (sometimes called 'guided fantasy'). The idea is that you suggest a series of situations and the class write down what ideas and images occur to them. For example, imagine a room and describe it: there is a piece of furniture that draws your attention, what is it? a newspaper is lying on a table: what date is on the newspaper? what is the headline? what is the view from the window? what noise do you hear? what does it remind you of? And so on. I give the pupils about a dozen questions then tell them to use their answers as material for a first draft of a poem. Sometimes they will write poems using all the answers in order, sometimes it is one question and its answer that forms the basis of the whole poem. The great advantage of structured writing is that it gives everyone a first draft and avoids the complaint, 'I can't think of anything to write'.

Freeze frame

Another way of using visual stimulus, which also uses a series of questions, came to me while I was running a 'Science and Poetry' session with a group of Year 6 children who were about to join our secondary school. The Science teacher played videos of a spark plug, and of the chrome on a bicycle, gradually being magnified thousands of times. The videos, only a few minutes each, were truly amazing; the change of textures were unbelievable. Each 'finished' with the screen filled with light.

What I did was replay the videos using the remote control to 'freeze' the images every few seconds. Whenever I did this, I told pupils to write down what they could see, what they had just seen, and/or what it reminded them of. The poems were full of bold contrasts, moving from huge landscape to the local and familiar. I would happily recommend this exercise for any age group; the Science department will have videos on space exploration or the natural world, which would be ideal.

3::THE THRILL OF WRITING

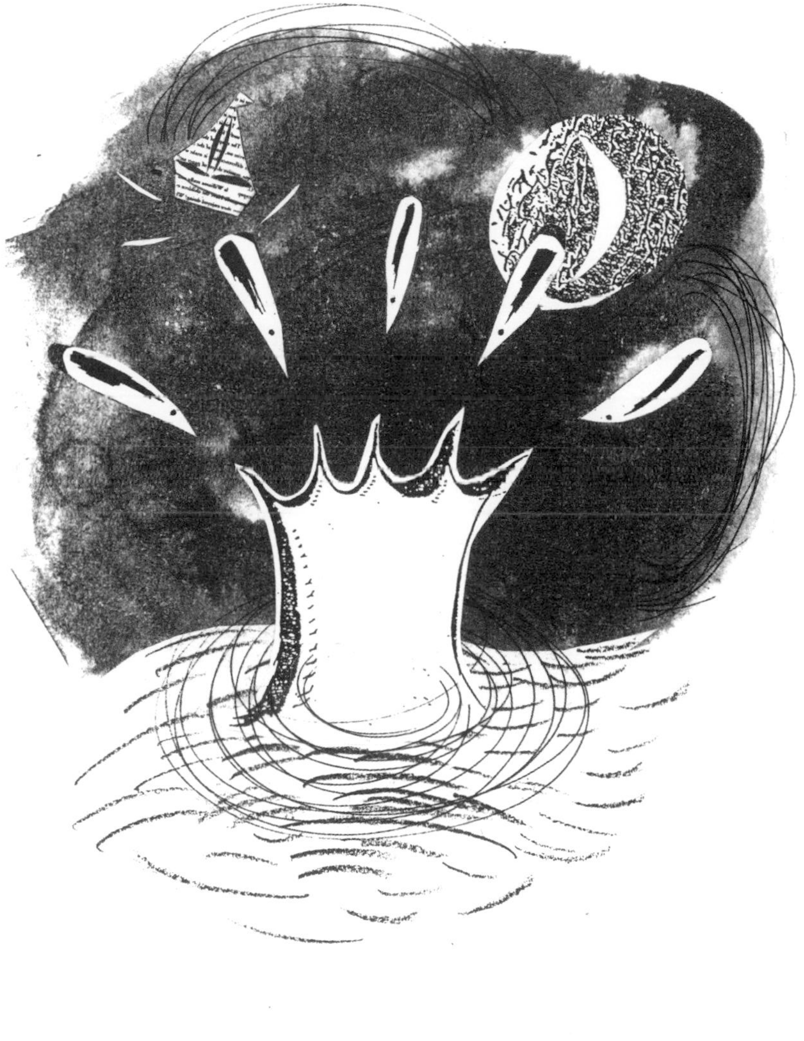

YOUNG PEOPLE NEED to experience the thrill of writing; ideally to become so absorbed in the process that they forget what day it is. In his brilliant book *Poetry in the Making*, Ted Hughes talks about the thrill of writing as analogous to fishing. Writing involves 'settling the mind', which Ted Hughes learnt from spending, 'hundreds and hundreds of hours staring at a float – a dot of red or yellow the size of a lentil, ten yards away', during which time 'you enter one of the orders of bliss':

> And the whole purpose of this concentrated excitement, in this arena of apprehension and unforeseeable events, is to bring up some lovely solid thing like living metal from a world where nothing exists but those inevitable facts which raise life out of nothing and return it to nothing.

How much time, during the lesson, should we set aside for writing, to develop this habit of 'concentrated excitement', and what are the benefits? As an exercise, Ted Hughes suggests setting strict limits – one side of writing in about 10 minutes:

> These artificial limits create a crisis, which ruses the brain's resources; the compulsion towards haste overthrows the ordinary precautions, flings everything into top gear, and many things that are usually hidden find themselves rushed into the open. Barriers break down, prisoners come out of their cells.

This allows young people to write what they would not otherwise have written, to surprise themselves by what they write. For this reason a brief period of concentrated writing is valuable in any poetry lesson. One side of writing may be too long for some pupils, but the time limit can apply to everyone. If pupils want to carry on longer, of course they should be allowed to. The important thing is that intense, focused time of writing. The aim, Ted Hughes says, is 'to develop the habit of all-out flowing exertion, for a short, concentrated period, in a definite direction'.

Instant poems

Apart from writing, what other activity is really important in a poetry lesson? What do we spend most of the lesson doing? The answer is, of course, talking.

Ian McMillan places a special emphasis on talk. I first met Ian McMillan when he came into Upton-by-Chester County High, where I was teaching. There was not much silence and concentration, but there was a great deal of talking and laughing, especially laughing. He made up poems as he went along, using anything that caught his attention: the name of the school, things that he had in his pockets, the books lined up on the shelves. Any idea that the children suggested was valued and used, nothing was ignored. He says, about his aims when he goes into a school:

> I want the children (and the teachers, the dinner ladies, the caretaker and the person who's come to mend the photocopier) to be excited by the possibilities of words to make you laugh until you cry and (occasionally, in my case), the other way round. I want them to be stimulated by the immediacy of anecdote and the daftness of rhyme and the electricity of memory and the silly names that things have.

His focus is on talk rather than writing, and this is deliberate:

> I've worked with musicians and visual artists and dancers: it feels after all this time that the immediacy of Talk can create a kind of instant poetry that writing simply can't improve on.

This excitement with the possibilities of language is incredibly infectious and stimulating. The effect on pupils' attitude to poetry is immediate. It encourages experimentation and taking risks with language, it makes working with words into something that is fun, desirable and exciting; this inevitably spills over into pupils' writing.

I am sure this excitement and delight in language is what Kenneth Koch is referring to when he talks about encouraging children to be 'crazy' in their writing. In his influential book on teaching poetry, *Wishes Lies and Dreams*, he writes:

> 'Another strategy I'd used more or less instinctively, encouraging children to be free and even 'crazy' in what they wrote, also had especially good results. They wrote freely and crazily and they liked what they were doing because they were writing beautiful and vivid things. The trouble with a child's not being crazy is that he will instead be conventional; and it is a truth of poetry that a

> conventional image, for example, is not, as far as its effect is concerned, an image at all. . .

Another way of generating excitement, that Ian McMillan makes use of, is getting pupils to join in performance poems. This is a great way of livening up a class and getting them excited about language. One performance poem that I use with a class (getting them to join in) is this one, that I first heard Ian McMillan perform on a canal boat in Chester:

TRAINSPOTTER

Trainspotter trainspotter trainspotter
Train train
Trainspotter trainspotter trainspotter
Train train

He's got the anorak
He's got the duffle bag
He's got the big notebook
And a pocket full of pens
Fountain pens and cartridge pens
And all those flippin' biros

And all those flippin' biros

Derek's ready
Derek's ready
Derek's ready
For the Red light
Orange light
Green light
GO!
WHOOSH!!
MISSED IT!

Trainspotter trainspotter trainspotter
Train train

Trainspotter trainspotter trainspotter
Train train

He's got the thermos flask
He's got the sandwiches
He's got the big bag of crisps
Chocolate bars and Yorkie bars
And all those flippin' Penguins

And all those flippin' Penguins

Derek's ready
Derek's ready
Derek's ready
For the Red light
Orange light
Green light
GO!
WHOOSH!!
MISSED IT!!

Missed it. Again.

Have another go
Have another go
Get a closer look
Get a closer look
At the
Red light
Orange light
Green light
Go!
WHOOSH!!

Ouch!
Caught it!!!

Right in the back
Right in the back
Right in the back of the anorak.

So now they're spotting Derek
So now they're spotting Derek

Trainspotter trainspotter trainspotter
Train train
Trainspotter trainspotter trainspotter
Train train

They've got the duffle bag
That's in Crewe
They've got the family bag of crisps
That's in Wick
They've got the big notebook
That's loose leaf –
Covers all the regions

Covers all the regions

Mind you so does Derek
Mind you so does Derek
With his
Red light
Orange light
Green light
GO!
WHOOSH!!

Trainspotter trainspotter trainspotter
Train train
Trainspotter trainspotter trainspotter
Train train
Nyeeeyaah!!

David Harmer and Martyn Wiley

Performance poems don't have to be funny, of course. The NEAB sent a tape to schools to accompany their 1998 anthology that included E. Kamau Brathwaite reading 'Limbo', his incredibly powerful and moving poem 'about' (among other things) the experience of slavery. The effect on my Year 11 class was mesmerising.

When I teach poetry, I go for a combination of moods and activities. This combination depends on the group, the time of day and the kind of poem that I am after. There is the settled time of absorbed focused writing. And there is also a time of talk and playing with language: making use of humour, anecdote and surprise.

Humour, anecdote and surprise

Not all poetry lessons have to be as funny as a performance by Ian McMillan. There are lessons when we'll want to slow down, work with a 'quiet' poem, and the mood and atmosphere will be more settled. Nevertheless, humour is useful, especially with a class who are apprehensive about writing poems. It breaks down boundaries, provides a relaxed atmosphere, and encourages creativity. Humour challenges preconceptions, encourages us to look at things in a different way. Like 'craziness', using humour in the classroom can encourage young people to get away from the conventional and predictable, to try out new things, to take chances with their writing.

Humour often comes out of anecdotes, and anecdotes are important because (apart from being one of the best ways of illustrating ideas and 'getting through' to a class), they allow young people to use their own voice in the classroom. Whatever their level of ability with the written word, however disaffected they are, pupils have stories to tell. Ian McMillan describes how he works with Year 11 pupils excluded from mainstream school. He says that although they take readily to visual art and the recording studio, 'words somehow don't seem glamorous, even though they use them all the time and they're very inventive in their insults, their gags and their descriptions of what happened to them last night'.

I noticed this when I worked in what was considered to be a 'difficult' school. The most demanding pupils, for many teachers, tended to be disaffected Year 10 and 11 boys. I remember asking one teacher what he'd done with his group last period Friday and he said, 'I got them to stay in their seats'. He was half-joking; he was a really good teacher. But only half-joking: these lads hated doing one thing for any length of time, including sitting down. (Another advantage of the 10 minute concentrated writing...) What they lads were good at was talking: their anecdotes could be hugely entertaining. Ian McMillan builds on this inventiveness by using stories:

> We sit in a group and make group poems about mythical characters; I ask them to tell me about the weirdest thing that ever happened to them, and for that moment it's magic: one of them told a fantastic, possibly made up story about being pursued by a police helicopter through some fields; one of them told a story that felt like a folk tale or an urban myth about walking home from the sports centre and seeing the same man over and over again, popping up in the unlikeliest settings ('and he were there!').

Asking for stories about the weirdest things that have happened is making use of surprise, which for me is one of the most fundamental ways into writing. Using the unexpected encourages pupils to think creatively, to come up with something new. Surprise can come from something brought into the classroom, like a canvas bag that is incredibly heavy ('what is in it?'), or from a sudden change in direction or activity; something unexpected that encourages the class to think in a different way. It can arise from writing games, which enable students to write things that they would not otherwise have written. I encourage students to surprise me and, as I said earlier, to surprise themselves. And good poems, of course, contain the element of surprise:

MIDNIGHT SHIFT

I listen to the crickets and hear
the machinery at the bottom of the night.

They are all made in Hong Kong
out of interchangeable parts.

They all raise and fall on the same wave,
the creaking, changeless sea
they made out of sand and the night air.
I don't surprise myself anymore:

a sense of motion but no advance, no shore
in sight other than sleep; and the usual
lines scribbled on the way, the notes
an alchemist hears adrift in the ordinary
with no symbol for the element of surprise.

– But then to feel your hand instead, palm up
on the bed like a little boat in the dark,

with everything calm for an instant
before out of nowhere all of you lands
on me with a great laugh, a splash of hair.

Paul Violi

4::MAKING THE FAMILIAR STRANGE

AS A STUDENT on teaching practice I was mooching through a book shop in Swansea wondering what I was going to teach on Monday morning when I came across 'In the Glassroom' by Roger McGough. I could see straight away that this was going to be tremendously useful: it is 'relevant', direct, funny and challenging. I wasn't disappointed. One of the first poems I still do with Year 7 (though I've also used it with older pupils) is from this collection:

FIRST DAY AT SCHOOL

A millionbillionwillion miles from home
Waiting for the bell to go. (To go where?)
Why are they all so big, other children?
So noisy? So much at home they
must have been born in uniform.
Lived all their lives in playgrounds.
Spent the years inventing games
that don't let me in. Games
that are rough, that swallow you up.

And the railings.
All around, the railings.
Are they to keep out wolves and monsters?
Things that carry off and eat children?
Things you don't take sweets from?
Perhaps they're to stop us getting out.
Running away from the lessins. Lessin.
What does a lessin look like?
Sounds small and slimy.
They keep them in glassrooms.
Whole rooms made out of glass. Imagine.

I wish I could remember my name.
Mummy said it would come in useful.
Like wellies. When there's puddles.
Yellowwellies. I wish she was here.
I think my name is sewn on somewhere.

Perhaps the teacher will read it for me.
Tea-cher. The one who makes the tea.

Roger McGough

THINGS TO DO WITH A POEM

Things to do with a poem: prepared reading

One of the ways I approach 'First Day at School' is to divide the class into groups and get them to prepare group readings. They divide the poem up in any way that they like, but the aim must be to make the meaning clear. This is a useful way into a poem; the readers will automatically have to make decisions about meaning and tone. In dividing the poem up, they become more aware of the complexities of structure: the structure imposed by form such as line breaks and stanzas, and the structure imposed by punctuation. The advantage of getting each group to prepare the same poem is that afterwards you can discuss which readings were particularly effective and why; their next readings will be so much better.

Having just started secondary school, Year 7 are able to identify with the discomfort of the character in the poem, and at the same time they have the sophistication to be able to find it entertaining. It would clearly be a difficult poem for children actually starting Primary school. Most of the things you would have difficulty explaining to younger children are those things which Year 7 will immediately find funny; 'Tea-cher. The one who makes the tea.' For this reason, the poem provides a useful way into talking about irony, and language.

The narrator's difficulties with life at school are partly about difficulties with language: he has forgotten his name and can't read it, he doesn't understand the meaning of 'tea-cher', 'glassroom' or 'lessin'. The words that he finds difficult are words that are usually considered familiar and ordinary. 'First Day at School' makes the familiar appear strange.

MY LIFE ASLEEP

Everything is loud: the rasp of the bed-sheets,
clamour of hair-tangles, clink of teeth.
Small sweat takes up residence in each crease
of the body, but breathing's even, herself warm,

room safe as a London room can be.
The tube rumbles only metres underneath
and planes for Heathrow circle on the roof.
You'll find the body and all the air it exhales
smellier than by day; she's kinder, more supple.
Bend close to catch the delicacies of sleep,
to hear skin tick, to taste the mandragora
of night sweat. Lean forward and put a finger
on the spot you think the dream is.

Jo Shapcott

Jo Shapcott writes:

I live in London in a part of the city which is never quiet even at night. This led me first of all to wonder if my sleep was especially shallow; then to wonder further what I looked like asleep, was I more than usually restless, for example? And finally, I began to be curious about who or what I was when I was asleep. What was my life like as a sleeping person? These are things which I could never know in reality, of course, but could reach towards in a poem. Broader questions of identity and humanity inevitably emerge once you start asking yourself this sort of thing. I often find asking a series of questions about seemingly everyday things can kick start a poem and take it into wonderfully unexpected territory. Taking this poem as a model, some of my students have written their own lives asleep, all surprisingly different. I ask them to use every one of their five senses, so that smell, sound, taste and touch enliven the poems as well as vision. Being tougher on them than I was on myself, for the purposes of this exercise I always ban that tempting word 'dream'.

One of the most popular exhortations of English teachers is to encourage students to use their senses in their writing, and a standard assignment is to ask pupils to imagine they are waking up in the morning and then writing down the first things that they hear. Jo Shapcott's poem gives a whole new angle on this.

Her point about 'asking a series of questions about seemingly everyday things' is also useful, not only as a starting point for a poem, but also at the drafting stage of any poem. 'My Life Asleep' like 'First Day at School' makes the familiar strange: it takes a seemingly everyday (everynight) subject and turns it into something astonishing.

What am I?

Making the familiar seem strange is true of a great deal of poetry, including riddles. Year 7 will be used to riddles from Key Stage 2 but may not have read these striking examples translated from the Serbo-Croat which can be found in *The Golden Apple* by Vasko Popa:

WINTER
No teeth, no hands, but it still bites.

SNOW
I flew like an eagle, fell like a king, died like a dog.

HEAD
Pot with seven holes
Pour water in and it doesn't run out.

CORPSE AND BEARERS
Five bodies, four souls and a hundred nails.

NEEDLE
I am young and slender
When I travel I have no tail
The further I go
The less there is of my tail
I lose it as I go
And come home tailless.

TROUSERS
I jumped into a pit
And came out at two gates.

I have used these with all ages. Try them out on a class, withholding the titles. In these riddles, the 'answer' is given in the title, which throws attention onto the way in which they are written. This is useful to explain; the point of a riddle is in the ingenuity of the telling. The best bit, for me, is in that moment before you 'get it', that feeling when the mind is searching for the answer.

Get it?

This notion of 'getting it', applies, in a sense, to all poems. Sometimes you read a poem to a class and someone says, 'I don't get it' as if it's a joke and they haven't comprehended the punch line. Just give it time, I tell them, the moment before you 'get it' is also part of the pleasure (the Serbo-Croat riddles are so difficult that your class will have plenty of time to savour this moment for themselves). One analogy is the pleasure of anticipation, that delicious sensation relished by Madeline in the scene from the film *Gregory's Girl*. Gregory is sitting in the cafe with his younger sister:

> MADELINE: A ginger beer and lime juice with ice cream please, but don't stir it [...] .
>
> GREGORY: That looks nice. Is it?
>
> MADELINE: Is it? [Toying with her drink] The nicest part is just before you taste it. Your mouth goes all tingly. But that can't go on forever.
>
> **from *Gregory's Girl* by Bill Forsyth**

Students need to learn how to read poems, they need to learn that poems don't offer up their meaning as easily as prose. A great deal of the resistance against poems that I've encountered is because pupils have not learned how to approach them, how to savour the process of 'getting it' and how to tolerate and enjoy the process of not being able to 'get it'. The very elusiveness can be a pleasure. As English teachers we know that there are some poems that you never fully 'get', that you can enjoy partly because of their mystery and strangeness. I remember reading Hart Crane as part of a course in American Poetry at Swansea University. It was like a kind of shared secret, these marvellous, dense, obscure poems.

I think it's important to share this experience with a class, and sometimes read with them poems that they will find 'difficult' and show them how to enjoy them, to delight in their strangeness. This works against the notion of the exam, where students are encouraged to come up with the required answer, the required reading of a poem. We can teach well within the exam system, but I also think it's important to take risks and try things out that would not usually be taught. One of the reasons that English is so popular is because of the liberating assumption that sometimes there is no one right answer, it's okay to discover multiple meanings, and to come up with something new and unexpected.

Riddles can be used with any age group and they are a useful way into talking about metaphor. The following poem is not a riddle but uses metaphor in a similar way to riddles, by writing about something as if it were something else. Unlike the rest of the poems in this chapter, it is more suited to older pupils (Year 10 and above). They will need their dictionaries, but it's worth it.

PILLBOX

Dome of the sun. So, we shall burn
Immured in a head, peering through hyphens.
Though we are prickly with angles of vision
An intelligence may calculate our blindspots
A hand rise out of the earth
To post us flames. Somebody squats
On thc skull with a trepan
Where our flailing glances cannot dislodge him.
The surf is placid at nights
And soothing the scent of camomile.
We have nailed this coast. Buried to the eyeballs
We shall burn like lampions.
The quenching Atlantic will back away from us.

David Constantine

David Constantine writes:

There are old pillboxes still along the Normandy Coast. They were built by the Germans against the threat of the Allied invasion. In my poem I try to imagine the terror of a defender waiting for that assault. He watches the sun rise and fears being burned alive. But the poem has to do with any state of bad anxiety. The anxious person is, so to speak, immured in his own skull. He is at the mercy of his own harmful imaginings. The poem is difficult, I know. The speaker seems adept at finding bizarre images for his fear. But that cleverness will not protect him and the fear is perhaps even worse than he can say. Or perhaps he makes it worse by telling it so curiously.

What is interesting about this comment is the way it demonstrates the layers of the poem; not only is David Constantine writing about a pillbox as if it is a skull, the whole poem can be read as a metaphor for 'bad anxiety'. Also revealing is the way he talks about the 'cleverness' of the poem, making it worse for the speaker. And the notion that the difficulty of the poem is, in a sense, part of the point. I have got some very good poems from older students by simply asking them to write about something as if it is something else. Another angle is to ask them to write about something as if it is alive, to use personification, which is one of the main strategies of the riddle, as the following poem does. I came across it first in Kenneth Koch's brilliant *Rose, Where Did You Get That Red? Teaching Great Poetry to Children*:

LES ETIQUETTES JAUNES

I picked up a leaf
today from the sidewalk
This seems childish.

Leaf! you are so big!
How can you change your
colour, then just fall!

As if there was no
such thing as integrity!

You are too relaxed
to answer me. I am too
frightened to insist.

Leaf! don't be neurotic
like the small chameleon.

Frank O'Hara

One of my most battered, well-used poetry books is *Lunch Poems* by Frank O'Hara published by City Lights; it's small enough to fit into a jacket pocket and for months I carried it about wherever I went.

What I like about this particular poem is the variety of tones; it starts casually, off-hand, unpromising: picking up a leaf? 'This seems childish'.

Then there's the outrage and wonderment of the questioning and the tentative, 'I am too frightened to insist'. Finally, the last stanza and the audacious labelling of the chameleon as neurotic.

Kenneth Koch suggests writing a similar poem to 'Les Etiquettes Jaunes' addressed to something like a flower or an animal, asking it questions as if you're surprised by what it is doing. I take this further, asking them to address anything they like, animate or inanimate, natural or manufactured; a telephone, computer, desk lamp, spider, anything.

This is a very open, friendly way into writing poems. No one can say they haven't anything to write about because the subject of the poem is almost secondary; the significant part is the questioning, the tone of the questions. Its apparent un-poetic subject matter is part of the point: poems can be based on any experience and written in any kind of language. This poem sounds like someone talking, the poet addressing the leaf. Pupils find this tone familiar and accessible; using it as a model is a good way of building up the confidence of pupils. It can also lead to good poems.

Drafting: who's talking?

One criterion I use when helping students with drafting is that the poem 'should' sound like someone speaking, the person who wrote it, or the chosen narrator. If it doesn't sound like this, then there needs to be a reason; it might be in the form of a recipe or a letter. In other words, the writer needs to be aware of the sound of what they are writing, the 'voice' of the poem.

In the following poem, written after reading 'Les Etiquettes Jaunes', the chiding tone holds the poem together and suggests the relationship between writer and animal. It manages to avoid the sentimental by the use of detail and obvious delight in language.

DONKEY

As you shamble through
  the mud, it sounds
as if you have
  clotted cream between
the weathered cracks of
  your horny hooves.

You snorfle your
  ridiculous nose into
my pockets, as if
  you think you will find
thistles growing between
  the bus tickets,
old coins
  and sweet wrappers.

Try something more
  interesting, or exciting.
Tangle that idea into
  your matted mane and
fuzzy,
  dusty head.

Ruth Yates (Year 7)

The following poem was also written in response to 'Les Etiquettes Jaunes'. It illustrates an important principle: not to be afraid of using specialist language.

LOVE BALLAD TO A SCOTT BOULDER MOUNTAIN BIKE, 16IN FRAME IN METALLIC GREY/SILVER £625 ONO

Scott, oh Scott, where have you gone
with your chunky, grey
'Psycho' tyres, so precious
to me?

No more Shimano Deore LX
derailleurs, or Mavic M236
rims, Tektro brake levers
simple, easy to hold
I'm not on a diet
but I've lost 27 pounds
approx.

Now you've gone away
I'm lost in a flat land, clean,
without my double-butted chromoly frame,
what can I do?

Swim?

Ruth Hite (Year 8)

This is a good way into writing a 'love poem': ask students to write a poem addressed to something that they want or that they have lost. Addressing the poem to an object rather than a person enables them to use the register of love poems in an ironic context. Using specialist language, as Ruth Hite does about mountain bikes, adds to the humour and irony. Michael Rosen selected this poem for the *TES*, 'Young Poet of the Week', and wrote:

> One of the great disservices we can to in the name of poetry is to suggest to children that some words are 'poetic' and others aren't. What I like about Ruth Hite's poem is her relish for a much-loved object, a relish that comes all wrapped up with its jargon. You can hear her slavering over 'Shimano Deore LX derailleurs' and that cheeky little 'approx' in the third stanza kills me. There's a nice double-edge to being 'lost in a flat land' – it's a fine image of dullness but it would also be a great place to go cycling... if you had your Scott Boulder bike.

Young people need permission to use the language that excites them. There's nothing more depressing than thirty poems all about spring, full of lambs. Especially when they're written by kids living in inner city Birmingham (or Leeds).

I was talking earlier about poems making the familiar strange. 'LOVE BALLAD TO A SCOTT BOULDER MOUNTAIN BIKE, 16INFRAME IN METALLIC GREY/SILVER £625 ONO' celebrates the familiar, and the language of the familiar.

THINGS TO DO WITH A POEM

Things to with a poem: learn it

Some poems are so good you actually want to learn them. After working on 'First Day at School', I've had pupils quoting chunks of it, even though I haven't specifically asked them to learn it. They quote it with relish. They haven't tried to learn it, the language has simply stayed with them. There are strong arguments for learning poems:

> Learning poems by heart is often enlightening; you really get at a poem that way, and you realise there are parts of it you'd been misreading or had skated over altogether.
>
> **Peter Sansom, *Writing Poetry***

Many people talk about how a poem stays with you when you learn it, how you own it, how it exerts a positive influence on your writing and a wholesome influence on your life. One memorable method of learning by heart is to write the poem on the board, or on an overhead, and then read it aloud with them two or three times. Wipe off a line and get them to read it again, remembering the missing line. You carry on like this until the poem is learnt. There is something satisfying about the whole class learning it together, in a defined time. The most exciting part is when you have just two or three lines left, and panic is hovering about; the class can see how much they have learned.

5::NAMING

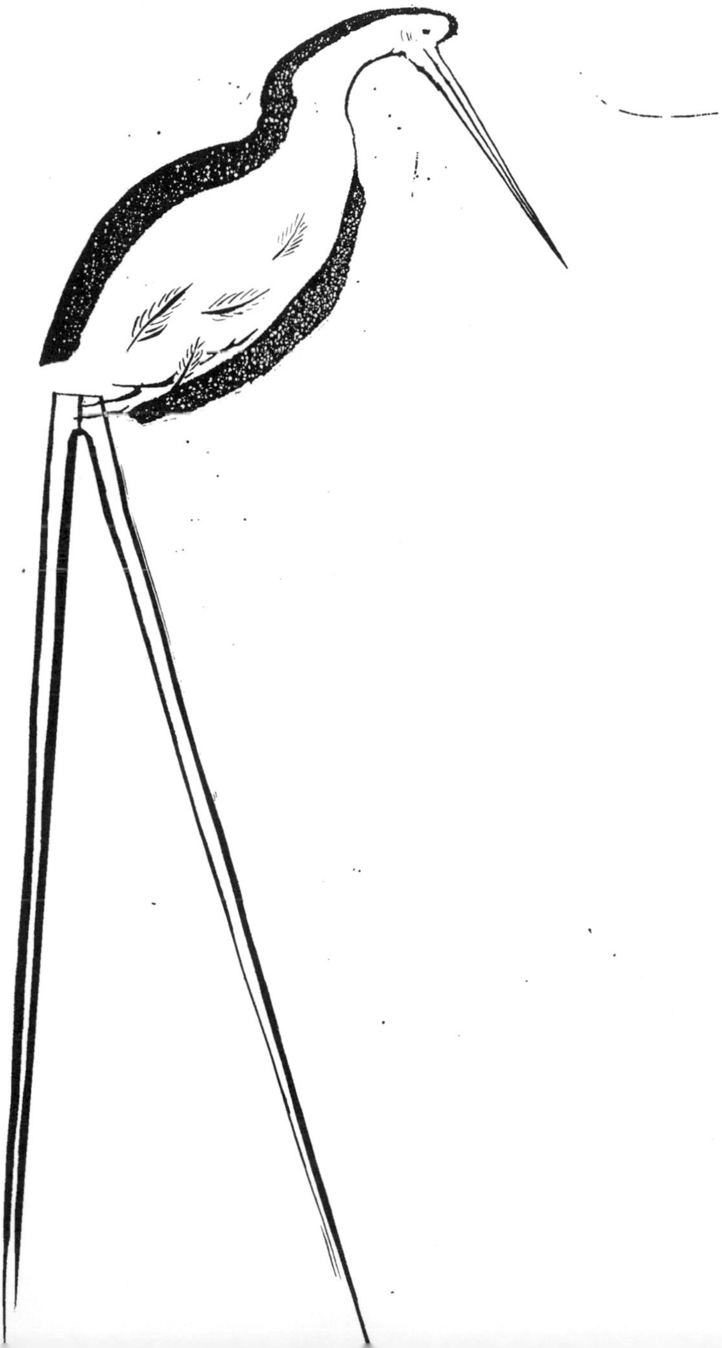

> It seems that in poetry, as in life, animals bring out the best in us. We are most human in the presence of animals, most humble, and it is only out of humility, out of uncertainty, out of ignorance, that the greatest art may be made.
>
> **Paul Muldoon, *The Faber Book of Beasts***

I HONESTLY INTENDED not to have a chapter on 'animal poems', simply because there is so much material on the subject. But the more I thought about it, the more I saw that I just couldn't avoid it. This is because young people can write so well about animals. Indeed, at a certain age, starting in the primary school and stretching sometimes into Year 8, some pupils would, if they could choose, write about little else. Paul Muldoon's introduction to *The Faber Book of Beats* makes me feel better about the whole business.

BAT

At evening, sitting in this terrace,
When the sun from the west, beyond Pisa, beyond the mountains
of Carrara
Departs, and the world is taken by surprise . . .

When the tired flower of Florence is in gloom beneath the
glowing
Brown hills surrounding . . .

When under the arches of the Ponte Vecchio
A green light enters against-stream, flush from the west,
Against the current of obscure Arno . . .

Look up, and you see things flying
Between the day and the night;
Swallows with spools of dark thread sewing the shadows together.

A circle swoop, and a quick parabola under the bridge arches
Where light pushes through;
A sudden turning upon itself of a thing in the air.
A dip to the water.

And you think:
'The swallows are flying so late!'

Swallows?

Dark air-life looping
Yet missing the pure loop . . .
A twitch, a twitter, an elastic shudder in flight,
And serrated wings against the sky,
Like a glove, a black glove thrown up at the light
And falling back.

Never swallows!
Bats!
The swallows are gone.

At a wavering instant the swallows give way to bats
By the Ponte Vecchio . . .
Changing guard.

Bats, and an uneasy creeping in one's scalp
As the bats swoop overhead!
Flying madly.

Pipistrello!
Black piper on an infinitesimal pipe.
Little lumps that fly in air and have voices indefinite, wildly vindictive;
Wings like bits of umbrella.

Bats!

Creatures that hang themselves up like an old rag, to sleep;
And disgustingly upside down.

Hanging upside down like rows of disgusting old rags
And grinning in their sleep.

Bats!
In China the bat is symbol of happiness.

Not for me!

D. H. Lawrence

'Bat' is an excellent poem for introducing imagery. With a younger class I ask them to pick out the lines that they like. This prevents them from getting stuck on the opening, which they can find puzzling. What they select will be the images. Ask the class what they think the writer feels about bats, and how they know. Lawrence leaves the reader in no doubt about how he feels at the end ('In China the bat is symbol of happiness. // Not for me!') but the most interesting lines are where he lets the images do the work, lines like 'Wings like bits of umbrella'.

This poem, incidentally is also ideal for introducing free verse. Ask the class why Lawrence has a stanza consisting of only one word ('Bats!') and the effect of this, in context. Then ask them to justify any other line breaks.

For a follow-up, ask pupils to write about a creature, trying to suggest, by their choice of images, how they feel about it.

MOTHS

In a daze
A dream taking you far away
Completely unexpected
Completely . . .

You freeze in disgust.
A tiny brown blur darting at you
The rapid sound of beating
Wings hovering above your head
Fluttering madly around the light
Like a desperate man dying of thirst
Like a drug addict – craving for more

Then – it's still
Dangerously still

You search the room looking for that thing
That – that MOTH

MOTH? A graceful word such as that, wasted on
Such a creature?

You can see it now
Its dry papery wings
Like an old document
Stained by its age
Camouflaged against the wall
Its black rubbery eyes
As you creep silently past
F R I G H T E N E D
In case you set it off again

A feeling of unease as you go
To wash your hands

MOTHS (MOTHS?)

Irritating ugly little creatures
With the gentle name

KEEP AWAY FROM ME!

Anna Bainbridge (Year 7)

I had told the class to see their creature in close-up, to look at its eyes and expression, and to use similes, as Lawrence does, to compare their creature to something inanimate, to suggest repulsion. 'Rubbery eyes' is unforgettable, and so is the 'dry papery wings / like an old document'. Anna Bainbridge also begins the poem in a state of uncertainty, like Lawrence begins 'Bats', which reinforces the sense of shock when the moths are introduced. I also like the way she writes of the 'gentle name' and its incongruity compared with the creature. 'Bat' has encouraged Anna to slow down and look carefully. She has also used pace and rhythm effectively, again learning from Lawrence's poem.

HYENA

I am waiting for you.
I have been travelling all morning through the bush and not
eaten.
I am lying at the edge of the bush
on a dusty path that leads from the burnt-out kraal.
I am panting, it is midday, I found no water-hole.
I am very fierce without food and although my eyes
are screwed to slits against the sun
you must believe I am prepared to spring.

What do you think of me?
I have a rough coat like Africa.
I am crafty with dark spots
like the bush-tufted plains of Africa.
I sprawl as a shaggy bundle of gathered energy
like Africa sprawling in its waters.
I trot, I lope, I slaver, I am a ranger.
I hunch my shoulders. I eat the dead.

Do you like my song?
When the moon pours hard and cold on the veldt
I sing, and I am the slave of darkness.
Over the stone walls and the mud walls and the ruined places
and the owls, the moonlight falls.
I sniff a broken drum. I bristle. My pelt is silver.
I howl my song to the moon – up it goes.
Would you meet me there in the waste places?

It is said I am a good match
for a dead lion. I put my muzzle
at his golden flanks, and tear. He
is my golden supper, but my tastes are easy.
I have a crowd of fangs, and I use them.
Oh and my tongue – do you like me
when it comes lolling out of my jaw

very long, and I am laughing?
I am not laughing.
But I am not snarling either, only
panting in the sun, showing you
what I grip
carrion with.

I am waiting.
for the foot to slide,
for the heart to seize,
for the leaping sinews to go slack,
for the fight to the death to be fought to the death,
for a glazing eye and the rumour of blood.
I am crouching in my dry shadows
till you are ready for me.
My place is to pick you clean
and leave your bones to the wind.

Edwin Morgan

The use of first person is worth trying with an animal poem, as a way of considering its 'character' and Edwin Morgan achieves this with uncanny precision in 'Hyena'. His combination of menace and a desire to please make for chilling effect. 'I have a rough coat like Africa' manages to be both outrageous and yet strangely appropriate.

A good way into this poem is to ask the class what they think of hyenas; this prepares them for the surprising use of first person; an unlikely approach, at first sight, for such an unpopular creature. Year 8 and Year 9 respond particularly well to this poem (though I have used it with older pupils). They like the use of the boast and threat, the hollow bravado and humour of lines like 'It is said I am a good match / for a dead lion'.

Ask the class to write in first person about a creature that is generally disliked, trying to make it sympathetic. The more adventurous could go for a combination of qualities, like the sinister and the ingratiating in Edwin Morgan's poem. Writing about animals in first person can allow young people to express feelings that might otherwise be difficult to express, such as self-consciousness:

STORK

I am hungry.
Razor-sharp beak
poised
to snatch
a silver-scaled trout
from the murky, shallow water.

I wait patiently
for my dinner.

I look down
at my thin, long legs
like chopsticks
protruding
from a feather bed
and feel

slightly ridiculous.
I hope the trout don't laugh.

Thomas Yates (Year 9)

It often strikes me how we make our choices about what poems we read and don't read in school. Also how the same poems tend to appear again and again in school anthologies. It is worth doing poems that you would never find in a school anthology, even if only to demonstrate that not all poems have to be 'like this'. Which is just one reason for including the next poem:

NAMING

Water
they unlidder
shrieve hurtled
folded,
suffixes – Dots. Dashes. Scraping fowls
Unescorted, Blade Goes Them

from a far orange –

DRAGON,

plum-BURR
plum-BURR
plum-BURR

Be come.
Be spoke.
Be eared.

Teal. Nor into
is drumming. Erred
bonnets alight: tattering grey Slackens.
Cause Doth
Middling shudder, squeal
Driven to Summit.

Bearings.
Oaths.
Mixed Pulses etched
Finningly, brilliant corners decapitate. Beast's
coat Loading
battlegivens: wound
Livery
laid into rivers, nails of
similarly blood-fine hatching
this is called/

fish.

Maggie O'Sullivan

Maggie O'Sullivan writes:

In my work I am concerned with exploring the oral, aural, visual and sculptural properties in language negotiating the textures, sounds, rhythms, weights, musics and silences dancing in the ear, on the page, on the tongue, in the

> mouth and in performance.
>
> For me, poetry is a process, an exploration of breath-word-making that allows the beauty and power of words to find ways of meaning through me: in this sense the poems are always beyond/ahead of me.

I read 'Naming' recently with a Year 9 class, to see what they would make of it. They quickly picked up on the use of sound in the poem and were able to talk about the use of invented words, like 'finningly', derived from 'fin'. I asked them what was different about this poem compared to others we had been reading and one member of the group perceptively said it works because of its use of sound, rather than 'meaning'.

It is an exciting poem to work with. It questions the whole business of 'naming'; 'fish' seems almost inadequate after the work that the poem does with sound. How 'correct' are the names we give things? Is there anything in the word 'fish' that makes it inherently suitable as a name for that particular creature? I asked the class to think of a creature, write its name at the bottom of the page and then have a go at writing their own naming poem, using sounds and lay-out like this poem does. Ultimately, the class decided, they needed to hear Maggie O'Sullivan's poem read, by the writer. And I agree with them.

Another poem that has the quality of wonder and a delight in language, though it is a completely different type of poem, is 'Owl' by George MacBeth. George MacBeth was the first poet I heard read, or rather the first that I saw perform; I remember he performed a poem 'about' Anan and Chichi, two pandas at London Zoo who were put together to mate. The poem consisted entirely of their two names, recited in such a way as to suggest their meeting and courtship, almost like a spell. It was unlike anything I had ever experienced. I don't remember whether or not the pandas found happiness together, but it was a cracking performance.

OWL

is my favourite. Who flies
like a nothing through the night,
who-whoing. Is a feather
duster in leafy corners ring-a-rosy-ing
boles of mice. Twice

you hear him call. Who
is he looking for? You hear
him hoovering over the floor
of the wood. O would you be gold
rings in the driving skull

if you could? Hooded and
vulnerable by the winter suns
owl looks. Is the grain of bark
in the dark. Round beaks are at
work in the pellety nest,

resting. Owl is an eye
in the barn. For a hole
in the trunk owl's blood
is to blame. Black talons in the
petrified fur! Cold walnut hands

on the case of the brain! In the reign
of the chicken owl comes like
a god. Is a goad in
the rain to the pink eyes,
dripping. For a meal in the day

flew, killed, on the moor. Six
mouths are the seed of his
arc in the season. Torn meat
from the sky. Owl lives
by the claws of his brain. On the branch

in the sever of the hand's
twigs owl is a backward look.
Flown wind in the skin. Fine
rain in the bones. Owl breaks
like the day. Am an owl, am an owl.

George MacBeth

This poem has tremendous energy and excitement. The rhythm and use of internal rhyme make it ideal for performance and the combination of this with the imagery is remarkable. He also uses line breaks to carry the poem forward and contribute to the sense of flight. I would give this a group to perform. It is also useful because George MacBeth obviously admires the owl and students do not always find it easy to write in this way about animals, without being sentimental.

THINGS TO DO WITH A POEM

Things to do with a poem: perform it

I once worked with a Drama specialist, presenting a group of poems at a residential INSET course, which opened my eyes to the possibilities of integrating movement with voice. One of our choices was 'Icarus Schmicarus' by Adrian Mitchell:

ICARUS SCHMICARUS

If you never spend your money
you know you'll always have some cash.
If you stay cool and never burn
you'll never turn to ash.
If you lick the boots that kick you
then you'll never feel the lash
and if you crawl along the ground
at least you'll never crash.
So why why why –
WHAT MADE YOU THINK YOU COULD FLY?

Adrian Mitchell

(Okay I know the rest of the poems in this chapter are 'about animals' but it's such a good poem it has to go in. Besides, Icarus was pretending to be a bird, wasn't he?) Our performance involved me leap-frogging off a chair over someone's shoulders and shouting out the last line. I will never forget the look on the face of the teacher in the front row when I jumped at him.

There is a tradition of writing from the point of view of animals that make a comment on the way animals are treated, as Edwin Brock does in 'Song of A Battery Hen', and Les Murray in 'The Cows on Killing Day'. Poems using this perspective can also deal with human issues. This one was written for me by a pupil in Chester a few years ago, and is 'about' the Falklands war:

ANIMALS NEVER FORGET

The penguins lie on the rocks
and stare out to sea.

The gulls sit on the cliffs
and stare up at the sky.

The sheep on land
stand
and stare at their feet.

The penguins remember
the big steel monsters, especially
the queer one that went under water
but never rose for air.
They remember the bright yellows,
oranges and reds that illuminated the sky
and the cries
and the screams of
the two-legged, land-living animals
who didn't swim.

The gulls remember
the strange, shiny birds
that dived and climbed
and spat fire
and crashed and exploded.
They remember the distorted faces on
the two-legged, land-living animals
who didn't get the chance to show

they couldn't fly.
The sheep remember
the big metal boxes
which made the strange tracks,
and the four-wheeled vehicles
and the flocks of humans
bewildered,
bemused and waiting
for the intimidating whistle
that would make them
into none-legged, dead, land animals.

Now all is tranquil on the islands.
But for how long?
Until the 'question of sovereignty'
is raised once more.

Alexandra Hopkins (Year 10)

Alexandra Hopkins wrote this after we listened to the BBC 'Poetry of War' programmes on the radio; poems, songs and other material. We also read a variety of war poems. I suggested to Alex that she could leave out the last stanza, but she decided to keep it. The endings of those long stanzas are remarkable; every one of them is strong enough to end the poem.

THINGS TO DO WITH A POEM

Things to do with a poem: compile anthologies

There are dozens of ways of approaching animals in poems and hundreds of animal poems to choose from. Compiling a class anthology works well; ask the class to find their own and choose what they like. Ask each member of the class to suggest two poems that they have read and say why they want to include them. The class can vote on which they want to put into the anthology. This provides a useful excuse for discussing a number of poems at once, and comparing poems that they have been working on. Ask them to justify their choice in an introduction, or by getting them to interview each other for a radio programme on the 'launch'.

Anthologies, of course, can also be of pupils' poems; the possibility of publication is obviously motivating. The process also takes for granted multiple drafting and detailed work on presentation. With a class anthology I would include everyone's best poem; an ideal culmination of a year's work. For a school anthology I would invite everyone to submit a poem and give a class responsibility for editing. Editors could select the poems, structure the anthology, and write an introduction explaining what kind of poems attracted them and why. Launch the anthology in assemblies or in a special evening for parents. At the launch, invite the successful poets to read their poems. This does a great deal for the status of poetry in the school. It could become an annual event. You could have a different theme each year (e.g. Animals) or invite poems written in a particular form, such as haiku.

6::THE EYE OF THE BLACKBIRD

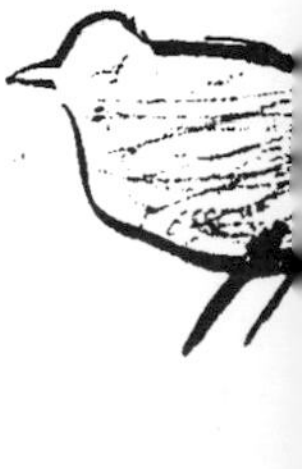

THE WAY I approach form generally is through the poems that we are reading; students learn best from good examples. If a poem is good, they will naturally be interested in its form. I don't teach forms for the sake of it; I haven't taught cinquains because I haven't found one that I like enough. There is an argument that students should try out a variety of forms and then they will then have a repertoire to choose the one that most lends itself to the poem they are about to write. I have sympathies with this argument but not necessarily in approaches that foreground the form. I generally prefer to foreground the poem; if it is good enough, pupils will naturally be interested in its form. I read 'Johnjoe's Snowman' recently with a Year 8 class:

JOHNJOE'S SNOWMAN

Johnjoe built a snowman
shaped like a wigwam
and postbox-sized.

What he didn't tell
was that inside the snowman
he'd stuffed the cat.

All Sunday morning
he patted with his shovel
the sides of that snowman.

He didn't bother with a head.
He'd never seen a snowman
that looked real yet.

How was it a snowman?
Because Johnjoe said so,
and he should know.

When it was finished
he stared at the snowman
and saw it wasn't right.

What the world didn't need
(apart from frozen cats)
was another white snowman.

In memory of the cat
he took the snowman
and sprayed it black.

Matthew Sweeney

One of the first comments they made was about the form; the 3-line stanzas and the repetition of the word 'snowman' at the end of one line in each stanza. This in no way interfered with their response to the poem: it was part of that response. They were reading the poem as writers and as such were straight away interested not only in what Matthew Sweeney was saying but also in how he was saying it. This is how they learn about form, by seeing it in action.

'Johnjoe's Snowman' by the way, has an intriguing, surreal quality, that keeps you reading. Matthew Sweeney convinces by the use of detail; 'shaped like a wigwam / and postbox-sized' and 'patted with his shovel'. It intrigues because it doesn't appear to occur to Johnjoe that burying the cat is not the right thing to do. There is the absence of guilt. Also we don't hear anything about Johnjoe's motive. Just when the reader might think that Johnjoe is maybe having second thoughts, ('saw it wasn't right'), Matthew Sweeney has him do something else crazy: spray it black.

As a follow-up, ask the class to write their own 'Johnjoe poem', in which a character does something ludicrous. They could write in first person, though third person can provide a kind of anonymity, or distance (it's not 'them' doing it, it's Johnjoe). Writing like this can provide a way of painlessly and playfully exploring the outrageous and the forbidden. On a similar theme with an older class (Years 10 and above), use 'Snowman' by Carol Ann Duffy.

Sometimes a poem has its own unique form, or structure, that lends itself brilliantly to students' poems, in such a way that opens up possibilities and truly invites imitation. One of my favourite examples is this:

THIRTEEN WAYS OF LOOKING AT A BLACKBIRD

I

Among twenty snowy mountains,
The only moving thing
Was the eye of the blackbird.

II

I was of three minds,
Like a tree
In which there are three blackbirds.

III

The blackbird whirled in the autumn winds.
It was a small part of the pantomime.

IV

A man and a woman
Are one.
A man and a woman and a blackbird
Are one.

V

I do not know which to prefer,
The beauty of inflections
Or the beauty of innuendoes,
The blackbird whistling
Or just after.

VI

Icicles filled the long window
With barbaric glass.
The shadow of the blackbird
Crossed it, to and fro.
The mood
Traced in the shadow
An indecipherable cause.

VII
O thin men of Haddam,
Why do you imagine golden birds?
Do you not see how the blackbird
Walks around the feet
Of the women about you?

VIII
I know noble accents
And lucid, inescapable rhythms;
But I know, too,
That the blackbird is involved
In what I know.

IX
When the blackbird flew out of sight,
It marked the edge
Of one of many circles.

X
At the sight of blackbirds
Flying in a green light,
Even the bawds of euphony
Would cry out sharply.

XI
He rode over Connecticut
In a glass coach.
Once, a fear pierced him,
In that he mistook
The shadow of his equipage
For blackbirds.

XII
The river is moving.
The blackbird must be flying.

XIII
It was evening all afternoon.
It was snowing
And it was going to snow.
The blackbird sat
In the cedar-limbs.

Wallace Stevens

Things to do with a poem: discuss it

One approach that works well is to put the class in groups and make each group the 'experts' on a poem or part of it. Their job is then to read their piece back to the class and talk about any points that they think are important. After the group have reported back, the rest of the class can add any further ideas. Give the class guidelines, depending on their grasp of a critical vocabulary; meaning, theme, choice of words, form.

This approach works particularly well with '13 Ways of Looking at a Blackbird.' Tell them to focus on what they can understand rather than on what they can't; there are no right or wrong interpretations. This frees students from the fear of 'getting it wrong'. They should identify, if they can, where they have heard or read the types of language before, for example the strange gothic atmosphere of XI, the reference to the world of geometry in IX.

An important point to make is that the blackbird is a relatively ordinary subject for a poem and is presented in a variety of settings. As a follow-up, ask them to choose a subject and write a number of short poems. The subject can be anything; a creature, an object, even a number. I wrote 'Fourteen Ways of Listening to the Archers' on holiday in North Wales; the energy of the poem came from the challenge of writing about something so ordinary and the sheer fun of thinking up a variety of contexts: memories, fiction, conversation, and so on.

Each short poem, or section, can be completely different, the only rule is that they should contain some reference to the subject, however inexplicit. This approach is particularly liberating because students only have to write a few lines for each section. It allows them to try out various poems and experiment. This playful atmosphere, in which they have permission to take risks, is incredibly productive for their writing. Sometimes one of the sections will 'take off' and become a complete poem in itself. Once they have used this form, pupils come back to it again and again.

There are plenty of poems that, if they weren't inspired by Stevens' poem, use a similar structure, numbered shorter poems on the one theme: 'Eighteen Plays on Golfing as a Watchword' by Simon Armitage, for example and 'Ten Ways to Avoid Lending Your Wheelbarrow to Anybody' by Adrian Mitchell. The form lends itself particularly well to poems that give advice or describe a process:

6 THINGS NOT TO BE DONE AT THE CINEMA

1.
Stand up and perform 'I am a teapot' with bright red clothes on.

2.
State to the person in front of you that their head is too big and
you cannot see, several times at the climax of the show.

3.
Make finger shadows of small frantic poodles run across the
screen.

4.
Hum the Batman theme song as loud as you can.

5.
Fire spit-balls at people with popcorn or drinks, in hope of
getting them to move and leave their drinks or popcorn
behind.

6.
Laugh a loud fake laugh at the least funny bit.

Virgil Scott (Year 7)

WRITING A POEM

1. Tidy your room:
you need a good environment to work in.

2. S P R E A D
your poem writing out.

3. Go round to Catie's for a discussion on
the world's major religions.

4. Invent a new one . . .

5. Hail great stuffed house sock,
I worship your mighty wooden stick.

6. Wear a hat to stop your ideas floating away.

7. Look round you and write all you remember
about it.

8. Alternatively just write down all you did
to write the poem.

Penny Buswell (Year 10)

Haiku

There are a variety of established forms that I use with pupils. One of the most valuable is the haiku; the economy and precision that haiku require is a discipline that will help them in any kind of writing. The essential elements of haiku are the use of a single three-line stanza with no superfluous words: saying a lot in three short lines. The more formal structure uses the syllable count – five syllables for the first line, seven for the second and five for the final line, but this is not essential.

The one 'rule' I will keep to, and this doesn't just apply to haiku, is Henry James' phrase, 'show not tell'. The words on the page have to do the work; if you get it right, the reader will experience the feeling what you are trying to communicate, without you needing to name, or 'tell', that feeling.

The best way of illustrating this is to quote some haiku.

The way I usually begin is by writing some on the board, pausing between each one and discussing them. The advantage of doing it like this is that the class have to read them slowly, word by word, line by line.

White lotus –
the monk
draws back his blade.

Buson

Such a moon –
the thief
pauses to sing.

Buson

In the melon-patch
thief, fox,
meet head-on.

Taigi

And the following contemporary example:

After weeks of watching the roof leak
I fixed it tonight
by moving a single board

Gary Snyder

After years of studying Zen and Japanese culture, Gary Snyder is undoubtedly closer in spirit to the essence of haiku than many of us. Some writers do not attempt to be. There's a tradition of having fun with haiku, as in this one by Richard Brautigan which is a healthy antidote to the tendency to take the business of haiku, or even poetry, too seriously:

HAIKU AMBULANCE
A piece of green pepper fell
off the wooden salad bowl:
so what?

Richard Brautigan

If you can say 'so what?' after reading a haiku, it has failed; a good test of any poem, I reckon.

I also give them Ezra Pound, 'In a Station of the Metro', though it's not technically a haiku. This is one of the only poems I remember reading in school. Our teacher explained that Pound wrote hundreds of words to describe his impressions of the metro; he eventually came up with this:

IN A STATION OF THE METRO

The apparition of these faces in a crowd;
Petals on a wet, black bough.

Ezra Pound

I doubt if the story is true; Pound wrote this poem while studying Japanese poetry. Nevertheless, the story does bring home the point about economy and precision.

TRANSLATIONS

There are many translations of haiku and sometimes I will give alternatives, such as these versions of Basho, (1644-1694). The first translation is by Lucien Stryk and Takashi Imoto, from the *Penguin Book of Zen Poetry*, the second is by William J Higginson, from *The Haiku Handbook* and the third appears in *An Introduction to Poetry* by X. J. Kennedy:

Old pond,
leap-splash –
a frog.

old pond . . .
a frog leaps in
water's sound

In the old stone pool
a frogjump:
splishhhhh

Up until this time, the frog had been the subject of many poems, but the focus had always been on the frog's singing, whereas Basho's frog is noted for the sound it makes leaping into the water.

Like frogs, haiku tend to jump; there is what Earl Miner in his essay, 'Ezra Pound; The Japanese Tradition in British and American Poetry' calls 'seemingly discordant halves' divided by a 'cutting word' or *kireji*. It follows from this that the second and third translations are closer to the original, in that the sound is contained in the last line of the Japanese version. The Lucien Stryk/Takashi Imoto translation gives a completely different emphasis.

You can give a class these translations and discuss the differences, or use them to write a 'translation' of their own. This can lead to useful discussion on translation itself; whether it is more important to translate precisely, or to write more freely in an attempt to give the poem the same impact as the original. Translation is a fascinating area to work on with young people and I have not got the space here to do it justice. There is an excellent chapter on translation in *Writing Poetry* by Matthew Sweeney and John Hartley Williams which explores this area and its possibilities.

Writing haiku

I ask the class to write a number of haiku in one session, even if they are focusing on one particular subject. Haikus need not follow the syllabic structure (after all, none of these do) though I suggest they try at least one as a way of getting them to question every word in a particular poem. I encourage them to be playful as well as disciplined. One of the great advantages of haiku is their brevity; this makes them ideal for drafting, few children will grumble at having to write out such a short poem more than once.

You can also do some useful work on presentation: show the pupils Japanese ideograms and paintings and get them to be as inventive as they like on a side of A4. One of the most dramatic and beautiful pieces of work I have ever received was from a Year 7 lad in Chester who asked me if he could illustrate Taigi's 'melon patch' haiku. I wish I had kept a copy.

One approach is to encourage the class to focus on something brought into the classroom, or take the class outdoors and let them choose a subject and write. Perhaps it's just me (it probably is), but the pupils that I teach tend to go for the jokes:

Bad spellers
of the world
Unit

William Marriott (Year 9)

Lightning strike –
Bird
Clings to its nest

John Ayliffe (Year 9)

Five years
seventeen syllables
floating down river

Jonathon Phillips (Year 9)

Jonathon Phillips' haiku is a response to a story I told the class about a Zen master who apparently spent years on a haiku and when he finished it, floated it downstream. It's a useful story to tell a class when they have written a poem that they are really pleased with and are worried that they will never write quite as well again. I tell them to forget it, just write another poem.

The following haiku started life as the first and third lines of the first stanza of a villanelle. Michael Tayler wasn't happy with the whole poem, but I liked these lines so much that I suggested liberating them:

I own a big shiny Lamborghini
when I go fast
it seems to please me

Michael Tayler (Year 9)

Liberating lines from poems and using them elsewhere is, of course, one way of drafting. Drafting is probably the most important aspect of any poetry lesson, helping people fashion poems out of their experience and imagination. However good the original idea, if the students do not know what to do with it, it's a lost opportunity. I have been talking about short poems in this chapter. The big advantage of writing short poems is that they are ideal for drafting, simply because they are quicker to write out.

Drafting: crossing out unnecessary words

I try to see students between drafts of a poem, give suggestions, and leave the final decision to them. What I try to do is help the student to say what they want to say. This may involve suggesting a different point of view, or suggesting a change in structure, or word choice. The most common piece of advice is to cross out all unnecessary words. To show not tell.

What do you think?

It is important to be positive but not to give praise when it hasn't been earned. There is always something encouraging to say about a piece of writing, but most students know when something is not good enough, and if you let them get away with it, you lose trust. One the things I say to a student when they hand me a draft is 'what do you think?' More often than not, they will be aware of the areas that need work.

7::MUSHROOMED

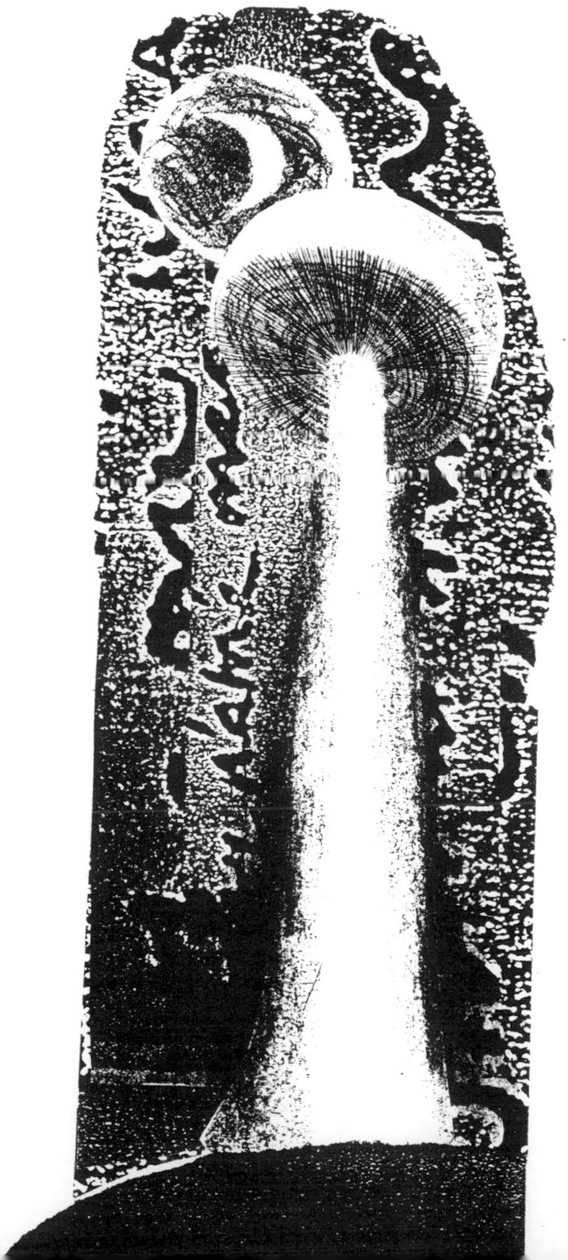

ONE POEM THAT I look forward to reading with Year 10 (or an older group if they haven't already read it) is this:

MUSHROOMS

Overnight, very
Whitely, discreetly,
Very quietly

Our toes, our noses
Take hold on the loam,
Acquire the air.

Nobody sees us,
Stops us, betrays us;
The small grains make room.

Soft fists insist on
Heaving the needles,
The leafy bedding,

Even the paving.
Our hammers, our rams,
Earless and eyeless,

Perfectly voiceless,
Widen the crannies,
Shoulder through holes. We

Diet on water,
On crumbs of shadow,
Bland-mannered, asking

Little or nothing.
So many of us!
So many of us!

We are shelves, we are
Tables, we are meek,
We are edible,

Nudgers and shovers
In spite of ourselves.
Our kind multiplies:

We shall by morning
Inherit the earth.
Our foot's in the door.

Sylvia Plath

THINGS TO DO WITH A POEM

Things to do with a poem: prediction

Give a class the title and ask them to predict what is going to happen in the poem. Thinking through possibilities generated by the title helps the class to read a poem from the point of view of the writer. This prepares students for the poem. It also makes them want to read it: they are inquisitive because they want to know if they have 'got it right'. Of course it's not important whether they get it right or not: a poem isn't a right answer. All their ideas are possible ways of dealing with the subject and will help them to appreciate the particular route that the writer has chosen. Prediction work is also useful because it leads to discussions about students' expectations of poems, even if these are confounded by the poem itself – multiple meanings, irony and metaphor, for example.

The success of this exercise depends on the title; it is useful for 'Mushrooms', but probably less useful for poems by Ian McMillan such as 'Stone, I Presume', 'The Force of his Storm Knocked me from my Stool', 'A Cliché Defines the Moment in a Poem about Language and Oppression'. If any of your class successfully predict the subject of these poems please let me know and I will send them a pencil.

With 'Mushrooms', I put the class into groups, give them the title and ask them to list a few possible approaches to the subject. Then I tell them to choose the one they prefer and write the opening of a group poem called 'Mushrooms'. Each group presents their list of possibilities and reads aloud their opening with a brief commentary on what they have attempted to do and how far they think they have succeeded. I only give about 20 minutes for this, so they have to work quickly. Setting a time limit is an effective way of removing tension; no one can be expected to produce a complete poem in such a short time. In fact, because of this it is often surprising how much they actually do write.

The process of writing their own version gives a class confidence when it comes to reading the original; they automatically make comparisons, and comparisons highlight aspects of the poem, providing a way in. The next stages I like to use with 'Mushrooms' have already been described: use the same groups to prepare a reading (this is the point where they have to make decisions about tone – it's really worth comparing alternative readings, focusing for example on the number of ways you could read 'So many of us / So many of us'). They then present part of the poem as 'experts', providing commentary for the rest of the class.

'Our kind multiplies'

The power of 'Mushrooms' comes partly from the narrative position, the use of first person plural. The anonymity and menacing 'Nobody sees us, / Stops us, betrays us . . .' , with its political overtones, its implication of enforced conformity combined with intolerance of differences, can lead to useful discussions on ways into political writing and the use of allegory. You can ask your class to write from the point of view of another living thing threatening to take over the planet. Another angle on the invasion ideas is that a class could take this even further and think of what kind of society would their subject have. Mushroom society. How would conkers cope? Pomegranates? Bananas? 'Mushrooms' also lends itself to parody:

WE HAVE COME FOR YOUR LETTUCE

We are snails!
We are united!
We will eat your lettuce!

On those cold
And rainy
Nights

When you humans
Stay inside
Afraid of the dark

We will come.

We are snails!
We are united!
We will eat your lettuce!

The winged ones may take some,
Smashing us on rocks
With their long pointed beaks.

Some may be trapped and drowned
By the alcoholic dreams
You leave for us.

But we will still come.

We are snails!
We are united!
We will eat your lettuce!

Many of us
Will be trampled underfoot
When you come home late from work

But these
Will only serve as rations
For the rest of our oncoming horde.

We are coming.
We are snails!
We are united!
We will eat your lettuce!

Jamie Scott (Year 10)

For months round here, we have been invaded by slugs and snails, thousands of them. So Jamie is speaking from the heart, for all of us. 'Alcoholic dreams' is a reference to the custom of planting a jam jar full of beer among the lettuce. Irresistible to slugs, who drown in happiness.

The form of 'Mushrooms' is useful for students' own writing. Someone usually spots the use of line breaks. 'We...' as the last word of the sixth stanza, for example. Ask them to try to argue why it is written like this, and to find other examples where they can make a case for a line ending and its value, in terms of giving emphasis and indicating rhythm. 'Mushrooms' is a good poem to illustrate the link between form and content, structure and meaning; the mushrooms appear harmless but are organised, purposeful. At first the use of line breaks appears arbitrary but when you look closer, you find the control: three line stanzas, (nearly) every line, five syllables.

THISTLES

Against the rubber tongues of cows and the hoeing hands of men
Thistles spike the summer air
Or crackle open under a blue-black pressure.

Every one a revengeful burst
Of resurrection, a grasped fistful
Of splintered weapons and Icelandic frost thrust up

From the underground stain of a decayed Viking.
They are like pale hair and the gutturals of dialects.
Every one manages a plume of blood.

Then they grow grey, like men.
Mown down, it is a feud. Their sons appear,
Stiff with weapons, fighting back over the same ground.

Ted Hughes

'Thistles' is an excellent poem to compare with 'Mushrooms': the poems share the theme of invading wildlife but approach it differently, Hughes' use of third person compared with Plath's first person plural, for example. Comparisons highlight differences and provide a way into a poem.

Things to do with a poem: comparison

Even the most basic comparison is some kind of tentative evaluation that can focus a class's attention on a poem. It is useful for enabling a class to talk about what a writer is doing. It gives them confidence and helps to counter the unproductive tendency you sometimes come across to regard poems as remote and inaccessible.

I sometimes ask a class to compare 'Mushrooms' and 'Thistles' without revealing the names of the writers, then ask whether they think each poem was written by a man or a woman. They tend to get it right. This leads to useful work on assumptions about gender. They are naturally intrigued to hear that the two poems were written when Ted Hughes and Sylvia Plath were married. It's good for pupils to see that poets are influenced by one another, just as they themselves are influenced by the poems they read.

Line breaks

Talking about 'Mushrooms' I said how the poem provides a good opportunity to talk about line breaks. This is true of many poems. Line breaks are so fundamental that it's always useful to look at how individual writers make use of them. It is line breaks that help to make a poem a poem (unless it's a prose poem). What else defines a poem? One exercise that alerts students to this valuable and inexhaustible question is this one.

Things to do with a poem: poem as prose

Give a class a poem that you have typed out as prose, discuss it as a piece of writing and see how long it takes for them to identify it as a poem. This leads to all kinds of useful points on the distinction between prose and poetry and the assumptions that we bring to each. You should only get away with this once with each class. Also it 'works' best with certain kinds of poems. Pupils would not necessarily identify 'This Is Just To Say' as a poem, for example. It's worth discussing with the class which kinds of poem that it does work with, and why.

> ... there exists at our disposal no tool of the poetic craft more important, none

> that yields more subtle and precise effects, than the line-break if it is properly understood.
>
> **Denise Levertov, *On the Function of the Line***

When the students guess that your piece of prose is a poem in disguise, get them in groups to put in the line breaks. Or as a separate exercise, type out a poem but change the line breaks; type a few alternatives, including the poet's choice, and discuss which is most effective. This is incredibly useful for students' own writing; they will pay far more attention to line breaks in their next poem. Or discuss the second stanza of this poem:

TO A POOR OLD WOMAN

munching a plum on
the street a paper bag
of them in her hand

They taste good to her
They taste good
to her. They taste
good to her

You can see it by
the way she gives herself
to the one half
sucked out in her hand

Comforted
a solace of ripe plums
seeming to fill the air
They taste good to her

William Carlos Williams

Prose into poem: found poems

Another approach that highlights line breaks is to give the class a piece of prose and ask them to lay it out as a poem, putting in line breaks and stanza breaks. Tell them it is fine to leave out words; the aim is to write a poem that makes use of lay-out to add to the impact of the text. They could do this in groups and present the resulting 'poem' to the rest of the class, justifying their decisions. You can tell the class that they are in fact writing 'found poems': poems made from other texts.

Once they have done this exercise, you can get them to 'find' their own poems. The advantage of these is that it frees students from having to invent the content of the poem and allows them to concentrate solely on form. Give them complete freedom to 'find' poems; encourage them to look in all types of text, not only fiction but also advertisements, newspapers, and so on. They can also use overheard conversation. As real examples, show the class Raymond Carver's last collection, *A New Path to the Waterfall*, which contains poems made from other texts including passages by Chekhov. Another 'real' example is 'From Lorca's Letters' by John Ash, in his collection *Disbelief.* Here is one section from John Ash's poem:

> Now it occurs to me to write a comedy
> whose chief characters are photographic enlargements,
>
> whose people we see in doorways, –
> newlyweds, sergeants, dead girls,
> anonymous crowds of moustaches, wrinkles, and hats. . .
>
> and in the midst of all these people
> I will place an authentic ghost, –
>
> Marianita dressed in white, her hair loose,
> sewing the flag of Liberty.
>
> **John Ash**

In an appendix to *Disbelief* entitled 'Notes: Translations, Transcriptions and Mistranslations' John Ash explains how he came to write 'From Lorca's Letters':

> Virtually all the material for this sequence derives from *The Selected Letters of Lorca* as translated by David Gershator and published by New Directions. I had been asked to write a review of the book, but since I do not know Spanish

> and am no Lorca scholar I was unconvinced that I was the right person for the task. I began by filling a page with all the phrases, sentences and paragraphs that most appealed to me, and very soon forgot about the review. The Lorca fragments seemed determined to form themselves into poems. Some sections of the sequence derive from only one or two letters, while others are composed from widely scattered fragments. Once I had the material I wanted I did not refer back to the original letters but combined and rephrased different fragments very freely. As this process continued I added some lines of my own, but there is very little that is not related closely to Mr. Gershator's translations.

This is a fascinating account, providing a real insight in how a poem can come about. 'The Lorca fragments seemed determined to form themselves into poems'; it is true that at some stage of writing a poem, the poem seems to take on a life of its own. The interesting thing here is that the original impetus for the poem came from a different text, but when John Ash started to work in it in this way, it grew into something different.

Ask pupils to write their own found poems in this way; choose a text that they admire and write down phrases, sentences and paragraphs that appeal to them, then form them into poems, adding lines of their own.

Another way of making poems out of other texts is cut-ups: poems made by cutting up texts, moving them around and pasting them back together again to make a poem. An example is Adrian Henri's 'The New, Fast, Automatic Daffodils', a cut-up of Wordsworth's 'Daffodils' and a Dutch motor-car leaflet.

THINGS TO DO WITH A POEM

Things to do with a poem: prediction (2): a few lines at a time

This is an extension of the prediction exercise that works brilliantly with a strong narrative poem with a punch at the end, like 'Mid-Term Break' by Seamus Heaney. Write the poem on acetate and put it on the overhead, (or on an Interactive Digital Whiteboard, if you have one! I have neither, and use a whiteboard) revealing it one stanza at a time. Talk about each stanza with the class as you uncover it, asking them to tell you what is happening and to try to predict the outcome. You can put them in groups to discuss it and report back, or do it with the whole class. It's faster with the class and therefore easier to maintain the momentum. This exercise forces students to read carefully and fully prepares them (in this case) for the devastating climax.

MID-TERM BREAK

I sat all morning in the college sick bay
Counting bells knelling classes to a close.
At two o'clock our neighbours drove me home.

In the porch I met my father crying –
He had always taken funerals in his stride –
And Big Jim Evans saying it was a hard blow.

The baby cooed and laughed and rocked the pram
When I came in, and I was embarrassed
By old men standing up to shakc my hand

And tell me they were 'sorry for my trouble';
Whispers informed strangers I was the eldest,
Away at school, as my mother held my hand

In hers and coughed out angry tearless sighs.
At ten o'clock the ambulance arrived
With the corpse, stanched and bandaged by the nurses.

Next morning I went up into the room. Snowdrops
soothed the bedside; I saw him
For the first time in six weeks. Paler now,

Wearing a poppy bruise on his left temple,
He lay in the four foot box as in his cot.
No gaudy scars, the bumper knocked him clear.

A four foot box, a foot for every year.

Seamus Heaney

8::CONTACT SHEET

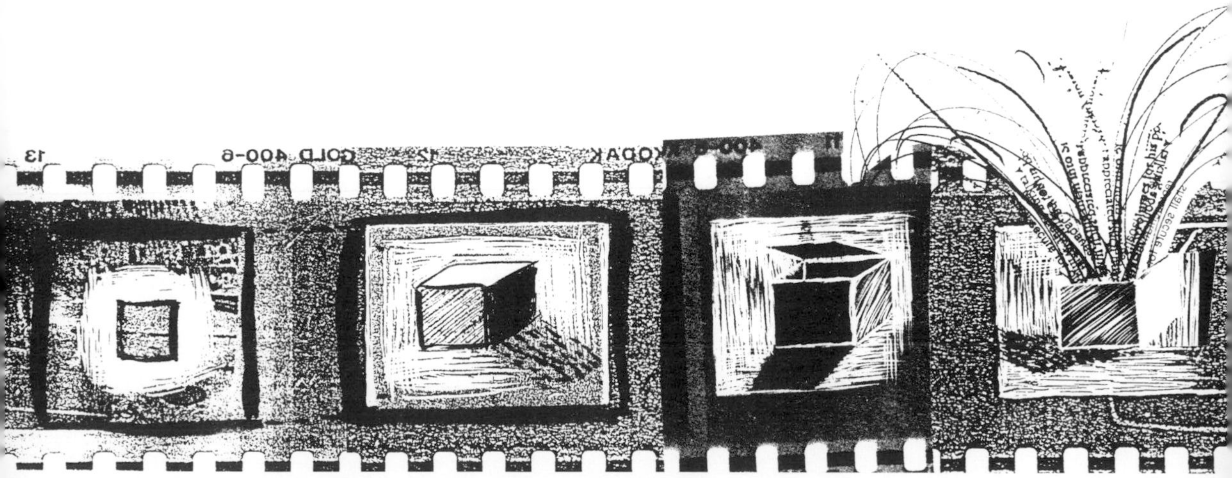

Photograph poem

The class imagine that they have obtained an old camera, one that they bought in a junk shop, or inherited. They get the camera home and find that there is still a film inside, ready to be developed; the last photographs taken by the previous owner. Ask them to imagine what each picture might contain.

Provide paper with film sprockets printed on it, the film divided into several 'pictures,' like a blank contact sheet. The pupils then write inside each picture six things that it might contain. These provide the notes for several short poems or one longer one, in which the photographs link together to tell a story.

This exercise was introduced to the Cheshire Poetry Project by Graham Mort who writes:

> The ideas of the 'latent image' is quite important here – i.e. that the film contains an image that has to be 'brought out' or developed. The process of note-taking, of making first drafts can be likened to the development of this latent image, which is then intensified, cropped and refocused, just like an actual print. The parallels between the writing process and photographic process were explored in order to de-mystify the writing process which lacks a practical vocabulary. Very often, I took students from the darkroom to the writing workshop.
>
> In the 'found camera' poem I sometimes tell the true story of being handed a camera which contained the last film taken by a man who subsequently suffered from the rapid onset of Alzheimer's disease – what were his last images and preoccupations like? This emphasises the fact that a poem 'shows' through imagery rather than 'tells' through narration. It also allows for the telling juxtaposition of images to form a visual narrative.

I sometimes take in an old camera as a stimulus to get the class thinking and talking about photographs. Instead of giving them the printed sheets you can get them to fold an A4 sheet 3 times, unfold it and write in the boxes. Doing something distracting like this just before writing can prevent them from worrying about what they are going to write; ideas come more easily when we are not looking too hard. Don't insist on six points for each photo: fewer can do the trick. Sometimes the notes written on the 'contact sheet' can by themselves read as imagist poems. Also, I tell pupils that it is okay to get carried away with one 'photograph'.

Existing photographs can also form the basis of poems. You can provide each pupil with a photograph and go through a series of structured questions, for example what is the first thing you see? what is just outside the frame of the photograph? what detail can you see? what happened just before the photograph was taken? what will happen next?

Using photographs, or the idea of photographs, is a fruitful way into writing about people. Another approach is to use imaginary photographs; they think of someone who intrigues them in some way and then imagine a photograph of them; first of all ask them to write down exactly what they see in the photograph, then ask them to write down the circumstances in which they came across it. Their notes can form the basis of a poem. I suspect Stanley Cook is writing about a 'real' experience in the next poem, nevertheless the season and the circumstances certainly 'fit' the photograph and what he is saying about it:

PHOTOGRAPH OF TENNYSON BY JULIA CAMERON

'The last and gloomiest of the Tennysons',
I saw your photograph in an exhibition
On a dank unaired afternoon
When the fingertips of grass were blistered pale
From touching the burning cold and the huge face
Of a peeling poster on nearby hoardings
Had two white uncurling corners below its eyes
Like falling tears. My own reflection
In the protective glass was no more alive
Than yours in the chemicals of the plate
And better than my observing you in the flesh
The early camera with superhuman
Accuracy detected the silver scribblings
On your beard and the beaten look in your eye.

Stanley Cook

This poem demonstrates another approach; the possibility of using real photographs of people. Get pupils to write poems addressed to people in photographs; people they admire, don't admire, or people they know nothing about apart from what they can work out from the photograph. They can provide an imaginary setting for finding the photograph, which 'fits in with' the photograph itself and the effect it has on them.

Another poem that I have used alongside the contact sheet exercise is 'Coltsfoot' by David Constantine. 'Coltsfoot' is not about a photograph, but it is a way of writing about character which makes use of a definite, clearly-defined setting. Sometimes I prepare for working with 'Coltsfoot' by getting the class to make notes as a basis for a poem. I ask them to think of someone they know and then write down a few words about a place they associate with that person, some detail that indicates a particular season (such as the weather), and a detail that indicates the time of the century, such as a song or a sporting event. I'll then read 'Coltsfoot', talk about it, and then ask them to write a short poem using their notes, addressing their chosen person as 'you'.

COLTSFOOT

Coming before my birthday they are forever your flowers
Who are dead and at whose hand
I picked them on the allotments and blitzed land.

David Constantine

David Constantine writes:

I wrote this poem after the death of my grandmother. My birthday is in early March, the coltsfoot are usually out by then. I remember them, bright yellow, in the allotments and on the bombsites in my childhood when I went shopping or visiting with my grandmother and picked a fistful of them along the way.

'Coltsfoot' is one of the most effective poems I have used in the classroom and in workshops; it is the kind of poem that slows you down and that you immediately re-read. It astonishes me whenever I read it for its economy, precision, rhythm and control. I have used it with Year 10 and above, including adults.

THINGS TO DO WITH A POEM

Things to do with a poem: write a neat copy

Okay, I know, it seems a bit old hat (handwriting practise?). In fact it really alerts a class to the detail of a poem. When Dylan Thomas died, he left behind a stack of poems in manuscript. Theodore Roethke described them:

> I noticed one day a big pile of poems – Edward Thomas, Hardy, Ransom, Housman, W. R. Rodgers, Davies and others – all copied out in his careful hand. He said he never felt he knew a poem, what was in it, until he had done this.

Writing out a poem forces you to pay attention to its detail. It also alerts you to lay-out and punctuation. It is important not to overdo this; it is ideal for 'Coltsfoot' but might not be suitable for the whole of the *Prelude*.

Box Poem

THE BOX

A tin box,
rusty, because it's old
and came from a junk shop.
It's like a run-down old person,
hinges squeak protestingly
when I open it
and there's an air
of age and time about it.

On the lid, 'Golden Virginia'
can just be made out
from under the rust
and the box still smells faintly
of tobacco, as if
it's hanging onto the past.
I can imagine
a musty, tweed-suited

Grandad keeping his tobacco in it,
or a grubby toothless
boy filling it with caterpillars.
But I keep letters in it.

They just fit.
A faded, pressed rose,
lightly red and sweet-smelling
special letters from friends, old stamps,
and sometimes, if I can forget
what's really in it – the ocean,
a grumbling ancient oak tree
and a summer's day.

Kerenza Swift (Year 9)

Kerenza Swift wrote this in response to the well-known box exercise. We talked about boxes of their own, or boxes they have seen, and what they are used for. The next stage was to write down a few lines describing their own box. It could be completely imaginary. They could imagine a story behind their box, that it was left behind in an old house, found buried in a garden or left someone in a will. Then they had to do the same thing as for the class poem; write about what could be in the box and what couldn't. They used these ideas as a basis for their poems.

I have used this idea right through the secondary school, including the sixth form. With younger classes you can have something in the tin, and ask them to guess what it is; you can have a smaller tin inside, with something inside that; a chrysalis, for example. You can have a piece of paper, folded small, and ask them what could be written on it.

With younger children I have demonstrated how to do this by beginning with a group poem. I took in an old tobacco tin, containing something fairly heavy. I held it up and passed it round, saying they must not open it. Then I told them to tell me what could be in it; they could include anything that would fit, however unlikely. I wrote these on the board. Then I asked them to tell me what definitely would not be in the tin; they could be as expansive and as daft as they liked. They could include the Pacific Ocean if they wanted. When we had a number of ideas, I got them to help me sort out the first draft of a poem, including the ideas they liked the most, taking votes about the first and last line.

With older classes you can dispense with the tin altogether, and the class poem and work entirely from discussion. Generally I prefer to have the tin; it provides a focus, and it's always good to have something they can touch. And smell.

Graham Mort writes:

> I've used a bag as well as a box because unseen interiors lead to the creation of imaginary worlds. It all started with me when a nine year old girl asked me casually, 'What time is it inside that bag?' implying some kind of parallel universe of the imagination. I've explored that idea a lot, moving from 'What could be in the bag?' (usually boring items like pens, pencils, paper rubbers, rulers, which act as metaphors for me, the writer) to 'What couldn't possibly be in the bag?' which allows for elephants, waterfalls, dreams, desires, time, space and the universe to erupt.
>
> I've used a set of three interlocking boxes too and the exercises to do with waking up inside them is often linked to Kafka's story 'Metamorphosis' – the idea is to create a fantasy out of believable details drawn from the reality of the boxes. So the details of the bedroom's sensory reality – smells, sense of touch, visuals etc. – are replaced by the sensory reality of the boxes. I always begin this exercise by the group handling the boxes with eyes closed and writing impulsively about the sense of touch, hearing and smell before seeing them and adding visual detail. I ask them to listen to their own heartbeat before and after handling the box as it goes round the group. This gives a kind of visceral urgency to the writing and pre-figures the sense of being isolated in a small place which I invite them to explore later.
>
> The boxes work as metaphors for imagination itself, for families, relationships, for towns, countries, the world, societies and the universe. So the notion that the imagination has to contain things, to grasp them is a kind of 'Tupperware theory of the universe', put playfully. More seriously, the boxes offer a kind of emotional safety because the fantasy allows students to express feelings of isolation, frustration and loneliness, which normally feel dangerous, exposing or volatile.

It's good to have 'real' examples of poems that make use of the idea you're using in an exercise, especially if they are as good as this one:

THE MAGIC BOX

I will put in the box

the swish of a silk sari on a summer night,
fire from the nostrils of a Chinese dragon,
the tip of a tongue touching a tooth.

I will put in the box

a snowman with a rumbling belly
a sip to the bluest water from Lake Lucerne,
a leaping spark from an electric fish.

I will put in the box

three violet wishes spoken in Gujarati,
the last joke of an ancient uncle,
and the first smile of a baby.

I will put in the box

a fifth season and a black sun,
a cowboy on a broomstick
and a witch on a white horse.

My box is fashioned from ice and gold and steel,
with stars on the lid and secrets in the corners.
Its hinges are the toe joints
of dinosaurs.

I shall surf in my box
on the great high-rolling breakers of the wild Atlantic,
then wash ashore on a yellow beach
the colour of the sun.

Kit Wright

Kit Wright's form provides an ideal model for younger writers; they could begin each stanza with 'I will put in the box', and later on use 'My box is fashioned from...' and finally 'I shall... in my box...'. Some pupils find this kind of structure helpful, like a container in which they pour their ideas. Once they have written the poem, they can experiment with shuffling the stanzas around and maybe taking out the lines they have borrowed from Kit Wright.

The combination of fantasy, 'a fifth season and a black sun' with sensory detail, 'the tip of a tongue touching a tooth' makes the poem particularly useful. It demonstrate how a balance between these can help make fantasy 'believable' and at the same time provide an imaginative context for their own experience. Making the strange familiar.

Incidentally, 'a fifth season and a black sun' provides a wonderful invitation to younger writers: invent a fifth season, with its unique alternative weather system. Imaginative Geography.

THE LITTLE BOX

The first box gets its first teeth
And its small length
Its small width and small emptiness
And all that it has got

The small box is growing bigger
And now the cupboard is in it
That it was in before

And it grows bigger and bigger and bigger
And now has in it the room
And the house and the town and the land
And the world it was in before

The small box remembers its childhood
And by overgreat longing
It becomes a small box again

Now in the small box

Is the whole world quite tiny
You can easily put it in a pocket
Easily steal it easily lose it

Take care of the small box

Vasko Popa

9::DON'T WORRY

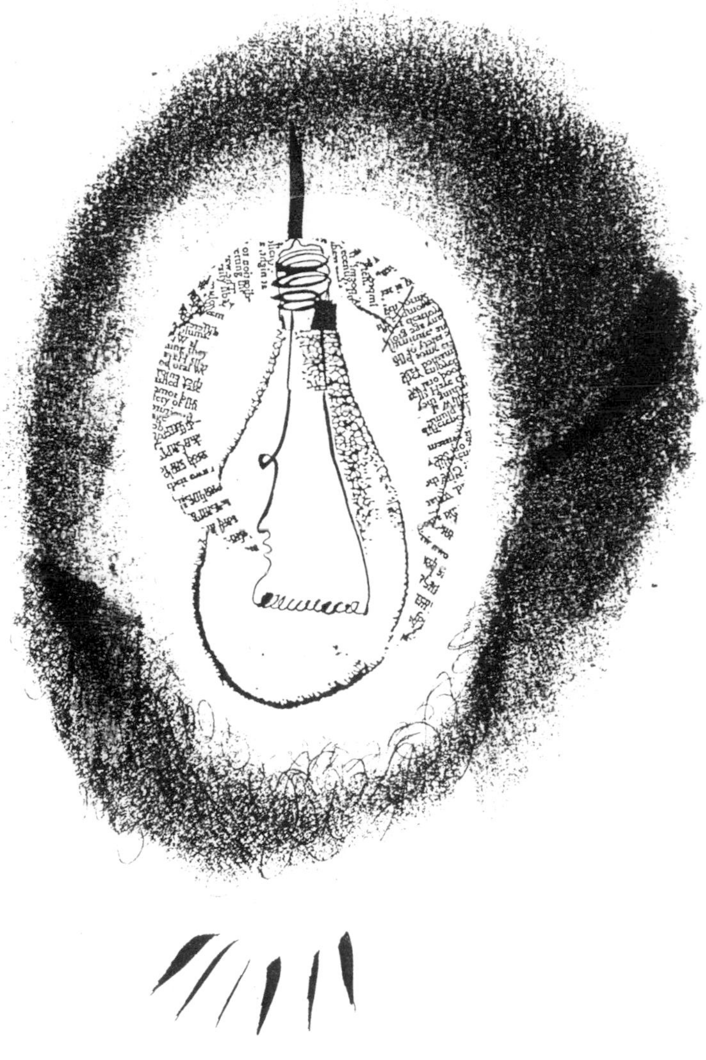

WHEN I STARTED writing a few years ago I started to attend Peter Sansom's famous Writing Days at the Poetry Business in Huddersfield. I still go. The effect on my teaching has been incalculable. He is one of the biggest influences behind the workshop approach described in this book. Peter and Ann Sansom have developed the workshop into an art form and are widely regarded as among the best writers who work in schools.

Q: What do you do when you go into schools? Are there any writing games or exercises that work particularly well?

P: We have a pool of things that we've developed over time. For example free writing. We give them a starting line and four simple rules: don't stop once you've started, don't rhyme because it's a constraint, don't write to the edge of the page otherwise it becomes a story, (so break the lines where you want to place emphasis), and most importantly, don't worry.

A: We always emphasise that this first piece of writing is private; they're talking more or less to themselves. Another important thing we say is that they mustn't worry about handwriting and spelling. As long as they're capable of writing something that they can read themselves, they're free to express themselves without any of the rules that might make them disruptive or difficult to work with. We're not asking anything from them that they can't do.

P: One writing game that we tend to use often is the objects game. This is basically a monologue where everybody is given a different object (or they choose an object) to speak in the voice of. This is liberating in a way that wearing a mask is, in drama – they're not writing for themselves, they are being a plug in a plug socket, a light bulb on a landing in a B & B. And because no one's been one of these objects before, they can't possibly do it wrong.

A: We often set it up before a break. We say, put this in the back of your mind, don't think about it too much. If someone asks you what you are, you mustn't discuss it, because they might tell you how you should feel and nobody can tell you that; you are the expert. When they come back after break they really believe they are the experts – they have that kind of authority. It's a liberating idea; nobody can tell you what to do.

P: Part of the reason it works is because you tell them more and more ludicrous things. Like, you're going to be a motorbike in pieces on the kitchen floor. It takes away pressure, no one expects to do particularly well.

Q: Do you write yourselves, while the students are writing?
A: It depends on the size of the class.
P: You've got to feel able to relax and become absorbed, to write. The teacher can't normally do that, but they can with a writer in the class.
A: I work with PGCE students in Leeds and they write all the time. They learn how the exercises work and how they can be adapted. They also learn how difficult it is to read back; which most of us forget when we leave school. I'd much rather have a teacher who is writing. If they're supervising, or watching, they're learning 'tricks', ways of making things happen in the classroom. They're missing most of it. And the benefit of the teacher writing with the children is immense because the teacher is seen to be vulnerable. And I think without exception the children are really encouraging.
Q: To the teacher?
A: Yes. It changes the relationship slightly; everybody is vulnerable and surprised by what they've done. And that's missed if the teacher has just been observing. The worst scenario, and this is rare, is when they correct a child or dismiss something that they've written; this can completely undermine what we've set up. It happens when the teacher wants the class to be a credit to them, and if they suspect someone is likely to be 'silly', they'll try to prevent it.
P: That's one of the reasons that we don't want specially selected groups. Sometimes schools will choose the 'cream' and they're not necessarily the ones who'll get most out of it.
A: They'll know how to please us. Often a teacher will say, we're keeping someone out because they've set fire to the school rabbit, or, he's having seventeen hours counselling a week and he's not quite ready. If it's left to us, they come in. Sometimes I find that the real 'hard cases', the ones who come in smirking, once they're given the freedom to say what they're not normally allowed to say, take the liberty of being tender or soft. It's often very moving. They are much more likely to surprise us than those who have always been praised.
Q: You are invited into school because you are writers. How do you judge the success of writing by young people? What are you looking for?
P: It's not a question of the level we work at as writers, and whether the kids write 'literature', it's whether the poems are alive or not, whether they're genuinely engaging with something that they consider important. There has to be some conscious shaping, of course, and this interests us more and

more, the way that we can get kids to draft.

A: I've been doing a project at Oakwell Hall where a school will send a class and we go round the park and write, and the following week I'll go in the classroom and work on the drafts, with groups of two or three. This is so valuable; they can comment on the work in much more detail. Also they are very supportive of one another.

***Q:** You were talking about the objects game as if it could be seen as a 'trick'. This leads me to ask what exactly is going on in the classroom apart from these 'tricks'. What are your basic assumptions, or strategies, behind getting kids to write well?*

A: From my point of view, everything I say to them is based on, 'don't worry, listen to yourself'. What stops you saying what you want are things like fear and wanting approval. Everything I do is based on removing defences, taking the pressure off.

P: And paradoxically that involves having rules, to give the conscious mind something to do. It's a combination of the given task plus the pressure, the energy created by the group. It wouldn't be enough to say, you can write what you like. You have to give some specific hoops to jump through.

***Q:** A structure.*

A: Yes. The other thing is the time element. We tell them, you only have two minutes to write this. No one can expect you to do anything wonderful in two minutes. In fact we give them much longer, but they never notice. It appears to put pressure on, and people really concentrate.

P: That's what is good about the Aldeburgh Poetry Trust down in Suffolk; it's a great initiative. Teachers come to a hotel, at half past six, to write. It's like the PGCE course; we discuss how exercises can be adapted and developed.

***Q:** Much of what you do is about removal of anxiety, allowing children to express what they wouldn't otherwise have expressed. Do you think that teachers working in the classroom can achieve the same thing?*

A: I think you covered it yourself when you said you worked as a writer; I'm not clear about what happens if you're not a writer and you're working with a group who are doing creative writing. I can see that there would be an interest...

***Q:** It's the practice of writing.*

P: Yes. Which is why I want people to write, because they'll understand something which is very simple and very fundamental but which is very difficult to believe if you haven't experienced it. The difference is not looking at the poem from the outside, like a finished artefact, but from the inside. It's a living thing, not part of the canon of English literature. The advantage in having a writer in the classroom is that a writer has got time to read poems, has been changed by the reading of poems and understands them from a practitioner's point of view, rather than as a critic or examiner. Often in the classroom it's the kids who are going to write better than us, because they've not done it before whereas we have. Part of being in there as a writer is that we can afford to show our failings. In fact they're encouraged by it. It's a wonderful way to make a living really, and I wish we did more of it.

More than a trick: free writing

As Peter Sansom says, this is an excellent way into writing, particularly for a group who are not used to writing poems. It can be used with all ages but I find it more useful with Year 9 and above. This is probably because they need it more! (I guess, for one reason or another, they are more likely to feel inhibited about writing.) Free writing is not something I would necessarily do on a regular basis with a class, though some classes would be happy to. Having said this, free writing works on the same fundamental principle as Ted Hughes' concentrated writing – a brief period of intense focus – and as I said earlier, this is one strategy I use with all age groups. Free writing is so important that it's worth reviewing the rules:

1 ***Don't stop once you've started.*** Sometimes students get 'stuck'. Peter suggests simply writing, 'I'm stuck I'm stuck I'm stuck...' which emphasises the important point that they have permission to write down everything that comes into their minds. Another method of dealing with getting stuck that I have used is to tell students to change the subject completely, just write about something different.

2 ***Don't rhyme because it's a constraint.*** This is a good opportunity to talk about rhyme. Pupils (and many adults too) are sometimes under the illusion that poems have to rhyme. Of course thousands don't, including *The Prelude* and *Paradise Lost.* Rhyming well is difficult. When pupils think of rhyme they tend to think of poems with a regular metre, usually a ballad metre. When you give them a poem that rhymes

without a predictable metre, (such as Simon Armitage's 'Ten Pence Story', below) it often takes them a while to spot the rhyme. They even say things like, 'Yes but it doesn't really rhyme', which leads to some useful discussions. There are some pupils who do have an amazing facility for rhyme and regular metre, but for free writing tell even those pupils not to rhyme, because when it comes to generating a first draft, rhyme is a constraint. For subsequent drafts, of course, rhyme can help generate ideas, and many poets use it for this reason. But often with pupils the tendency is sometimes to use words only because they happen to rhyme, which forces them to say things they do not want to say.

3 *Don't write to the end of the page otherwise it becomes a story.* Break the lines where you want to place emphasis. This brings us back to the notion of what a poem is, of course. For the purpose of free writing, getting pupils to make their lines shorter encourages the view that 'poems' can be written quickly. If they are used to struggling with rhyme and metre, this can come as a revelation.

4 *Don't worry.* As Peter Sansom says, this is the most important of the rules. If you tell them that you will not read what they write, that they will not have to read it out and that it does not have to be a masterpiece, you will have given them permission to write anything. Which is the whole point.

The opening line

To start a session of free writing, go over the rules and, when they are ready to begin, give them the opening line and tell them to write it down. The opening line is great for removing anxiety; the hardest thing about writing for most pupils (and adults) is starting off.

One advantage of free writing is that it can be different every time because there are an infinite number of beginnings. Anything can be used for an opening line. It can be an unfinished sentence like, 'It was just starting to rain when . . . ', 'Suddenly there was a noise . . .', 'The last thing I needed at this stage was . . .'. Of course these openings can be changed, for example pupils can use third instead of first person. Elsewhere in this book I suggest borrowing a first line from a poem as a starting point for a new poem; this can also be used for free writing. I sometimes glance through a novel to find a handy beginning for free writing. The opening of a novel can also be used. Like *The Long Goodbye* by Raymond Chandler:

> The first time I laid eyes on Terry Lennox he was drunk in a Rolls Royce Silver Wraith outside the terrace of The Dancers.

Read the class this sentence and give them, 'The first time I laid eyes on... he/she was...'. Another approach is to read the first page of the novel and use that as a starting point, taking whatever you like from the original and writing quickly, reworking it into a poem (by not writing to the edge of the page). To demonstrate that an exercise like this can lead to a 'real poem', here's one from Peter Sansom that was begun after reading the opening of the novel by Peter Carey which shares its title:

BLISS

Only laziness held him back. He could do
anything, when in that instant it seemed
there was no time. In the tin-hut Sunday School
he'd learned three score and ten, like all of us,
but he was shortchanged by tachycardia.
Beneath him the green rich-watered lawn,
the tattered banana tree, the frangipani's
dropped, still-dropping, single sweet flower
by his as yet undiscovered death;
all of it brighter than real, and seen by him
from above, like a film he thought
but no, more like a scene in the novel
the film is based on. Thirty feet up,
weightless, he stopped, not floating,
just being there. Though he always laughed
at the idea of an hereafter, the phrase
'Waiting for admittance' occurred to him:
a line in a song he knew the sense of
and the music, but not the words.

He looked round, it might be the last time

and, though his bifocals lay on the lawn
beside his book and body, he saw easily
the new estate: house upon house at which
Jimbo with that dog of his delivered
his late papers; and there was Mrs Deidre
hacking at her columbine; and there was Peter;
but mostly he saw their own verandah
where his friends and his wife were not panicked
or thinking differently about him, and no one
had rung for an ambulance. From this angle
how clearly he could read their shapes,
a language he had never known before,
the chiming just-touched wine-glasses,
the loose neckline of his wife's blouse
and how it was he'd come to marry her.
It struck him he could be here a long time,
his head filling with music, the soundtrack
to what he could see of everyone,
except it was not played music, but heard
the way some people can read a score
and hear it in their heads, and who therefore
never quite hear that music at all.

Peter Sansom

I first read this in *Poetry Review* and carried it around with me for days, re-reading it when I could get the chance. Peter Sansom borrows the incident from the novel, a little of the detail and something of the curious matter-of-fact tone, and makes out of it something completely new. It is one of those poems where there are so many good lines that you want to quote all of it. I really like the local, familiar but striking detail such as, 'the tin-hut Sunday School', 'shortchanged by tachycardia' and 'Jimbo with that dog of his' and the way it is combined with those long elegant sentences, such as the one that ends the poem. I like the use of humour too, the idea of putting himself in the poem as a kind of minor character, 'and there was Peter' (or is it the novelist?).

After reading this poem with a class (Year 10 or above, ideally 12 or 13), tell them to imagine an everyday situation, with their family and friends.

Then give them the line, 'Thirty feet up, weightless...' as an opening and tell them to continue it, describing the situation in the way that Peter Sansom does, trying for the same photographic clarity, using the same familiar detail. For this exercise I wouldn't focus on the theme of dying, just ask them to describe a familiar scene or situation (their own neighbourhood, friends or family, maybe putting themselves in the 'picture') from this unusual angle. Another example of making the familiar strange.

A further possibility is to give a class the first sentence of Peter Sansom's poem to start off a piece of free writing: 'Only laziness held him back' (or 'her', or 'me'). It's a great first sentence; I would never have dreamed about writing about someone dying following that. When using opening lines, encourage the class to surprise you by putting them into an unusual context.

An alternative approach is to give a class the opening of the Peter Carey novel and get them to discuss how Peter Sansom adapts it for his own poem, and then try the same kind of approach using the opening of a different novel.

The objects game

is a particularly effective way into writing monologues. It works brilliantly with all age groups and is a real gift for an older group who are not used to writing poems. Here is the complete list of suggestions as they appear in Peter Sansom's *Writing Poems*:

A vacuum cleaner in a shop window
A loose button on an old overcoat
A stained glass window in a derelict church
A lift in an office block
A motorbike in pieces on a kitchen floor
A wardrobe in a hotel bedroom
A spoon in a bedsitter
A bus shelter at midnight
A piece in a jigsaw of a landscape with scattered houses
A pub (P.H.) legend on an Ordnance Survey map
A bottle of aspirin in a bathroom cabinet
A safety match in a box in a cardigan pocket

A reading lamp on a tidy desk
A reading lamp on a cluttered desk
A roller blind in a window overlooking the sea
A paintbrush in a jar of turps

A BUS SHELTER AT MIDNIGHT

It's midnight, black as black,
The wind a bully stinging me with its cold,
The icy frost freezing every pane of my glass,
My light almost dead, flicker, flicker.

Then come the drunk purple-faced lager louts.
They crawl into the shelter of my structure
Deafening me with their loud cries
But I still stand strong.

Then it happens. They hit me again and again.
Thousands of my pieces
Scattered across the cold floor.
I stand in pain but who can I call for help?

Suddenly I see hope as the rays of light from a bus shine
Reflecting through me as if I am a ghost.
But am I a ghost? No one knows.
If only they knew I breathe and bleed.

Every night I swallow people and then spit them out.

Matthew Halsall (Year 10)

And here is a poem that could have been written as a result of this game but might not have been, about a light bulb left burning in an empty house:

A THOUSAND HOURS

There were false starts, but life, for me, really
began the night he unplugged the telly
and snuffed the pilot light. As last-man-out
he worked right through to dawn, between the street
and this bedroom, until he'd stripped it bare,
but left me in his rush to check the meter,
to turn the stopcock on a copper tank,
count stairs and memorise that manhole's clunk,
the first hawked phlegm, the way a window pane
was answering the early Lime Street train;
and posted back his keys to nobody.

I've hung here naked since, by day barely
able to force a shadow to be thrown.
It's nights I come into my own:
a halo for the ceiling, corners for mice,
and through the glass a phantom for all this,
a twin star that is shedding kilowatts
in translation. Beyond these dark outskirts
my creator sleeps. I recall how his eyes
would whirr just like this night-time visitor
that might outlive me. Of all his new ideas
I burn on, having been conceived in error.

Paul Farley

This poem is useful also because of the skilful use of rhyme and half rhyme; it demonstrates a possible form for the poem that your pupils can look at, when they are at the stage of working on their first drafts after playing the objects game. Alternatively, Paul Farley's excellent poem can be used as another 'way in' to the objects game. The advantage of having a variety of approaches into a particular idea, especially when the idea is as fruitful as this one (the monologue from the point of view of an object), is that you can come back to it again and again without the pupils necessarily realising it.

The following poem can also be used as a stimulus for a monologue.

The object is the ten pence piece, but Simon Armitage does not restrict himself to one setting. This poem demonstrates how narrative can be used in poems. The subject used to be a favourite of teachers when I was at school, write a story about the life of a coin:

TEN PENCE STORY

Out of the melting pot, into the mint;
next news I was loose change for a Leeds pimp,
burning a hole in his skin-tight pocket
till he tipped a busker by the precinct.

Not the most ceremonious release
for a fresh faced coin still cutting its teeth.
But that's my point: if you're poorly bartered
you're scuppered before you've even started.

My lowest ebb was a seven month spell
spent head down in a stagnant wishing well,
half eclipsed by an oxidised tuppence
which impressed me with its green circumference.

When they fished me out I made a few phone calls,
fed a few meters, hung around the pool halls.
I slotted in well, but all that vending
blunted my edges and did my head in.

Once, I came within an ace of the end
on the stern of a North Sea ferry, when
some half-cut, ham-fisted cockney tossed me
up into the air and almost dropped me

and every transaction flashed before me
like a time lapse autobiography.
Now, just the thought of travel by water
lifts the serrations around my border.

Some day I know I'll be bagged up and sent
to that knacker's yard for the over spent
to be broken, boiled, unmade and replaced,
for my metals to go their separate ways . . .

which is sad. All coins have dreams. Some castings
from my own batch, I recall, were hatching
an exchange scam on the foreign market
and some inside jobs on one arm bandits.

My own ambition? Well, that was simple:
to be flipped in Wembley's centre circle,
to twist, to turn, to hang like a planet,
to touch down on that emerald carpet.

Those with faith in the system say 'don't quit,
bide your time, if you're worth it, you'll make it.'
But I was robbed, I was badly tendered.
I could have scored. I could have contended.

Simon Armitage

The rhyme and pace of this are remarkably good. The poem also demonstrates another way of writing monologues from the point of view of objects: a poem in which the object talks about the life it has and the life it dreams that it could have had. The first part of the poem could be the story of the object and the second part, like Simon Armitage's, could begin with 'My own ambition? Well that was simple...'.

10::VOICES

Half an hour before the mutiny

In the last chapter Peter and Ann Sansom talked about writing from the point of view of an object; in this chapter, the focus is largely on writing from the point of view of other people. One of the main themes or approaches running through this book is the notion of writing in the voice of someone or something else. This approach has significant implications for teaching secondary school pupils. Young people of this age have a great deal to say but usually little 'experience'. They are also beset by complex feelings and emotions. Writing monologues in the voice of someone else, or of an animal or object can enable them to tackle ideas and feelings that they would otherwise find difficult to deal with. Paradoxically, writing in the voice of someone or something else enables young people to speak with new-found authority and confidence.

One of the best ways into writing monologues was given to me by the writer Nick Warburton at the Arvon Foundation, Lumb Bank, where he used it with sixth form students. The class imagine that they are on an ocean liner. The liner is a useful setting because there are no outside influences. Nick got the idea from Rose Tremain who used a circus, but you could use any location that has its own distinctive character, such as a school, hotel or railway station. The liner also offers a range of characters; the captain, purser, first officer, wireless operator, deck hands, rich passengers, second class passengers, a stowaway, and so on.

You suggest a situation where there is tension; they hit a storm and the radio goes down; one set of officers want to head for land but the rest, including the captain, want to continue South. There is a mutiny. You give each member of the class a character and ask them to write their thoughts half and hour before the mutiny, which is due to take place at the New Year dance. Also say that each character has a secret. As Nick Warburton says, secrets (and lies) are a 'spur to narrative': they makes characters more interesting and provide motive. You can add to potential conflict by giving more details about certain characters, for example have a rich widow and her beautiful daughter among the first class passengers.

Allocating characters can be done randomly, so that they might end up with a character quite different from themselves, which can be challenging. The focus of tension with the circus setting, incidentally, is that the circus wants to set up on a village green but some of the locals are against this and they have had a row with the circus manager. Following this, there is a fire in which the big top is burnt down. They should write their character's thoughts half an hour before the fire.

The interesting thing about this exercise is the way in which the monologues tend to tie in, sometimes quite bizarrely, as if the writers have been working together. Reading back is always an event after writing these monologues; the writers get attached to their characters and enjoy hearing what the others have written about them. Also the secrets themselves provide a source of entertainment.

There is possibly an optimum number of about fifteen pupils for this. In a class of thirty you can have two 'liners'. This exercise is not necessarily only for the writing of poetry, it lends itself also to scriptwriting, stories, and certainly drama. Having said that, I find it ideal for poems: the length is just right, and the elements of character and narrative belong as much to poetry as anywhere else. Finished poems can be displayed together or printed as a sequence. Pupils could also extend this by writing as if they were more than one character, developing their own sequences into a kind of poem/story.

Another way into writing monologues is to use poems written in the voice of someone from history or legend:

MRS MIDAS

It was late September. I'd just poured a glass of wine, begun
to unwind, while the vegetables cooked. The kitchen
filled with the sound of itself, relaxed, its steamy breath
gently blanching the windows. So I opened one,
then with my fingers wiped the other's glass like a brow.
He was standing under a pear tree snapping a twig.

Now the garden was long and the visibility poor, the way
the dark of the ground seems to drink the light of the sky,
but that twig in his hand was gold. And then he plucked
a pear from a branch, we grew *Fondante d'Automne*,
and it sat in his palm like a light-bulb. On.
I thought to myself, Is he putting fairy lights in the tree?

He came into the house. The doorknobs gleamed.

He drew the blinds. You know the mind; I thought of
the Field of the Cloth of Gold and of Miss Macready.
He sat in that chair like a king on a burnished throne.
The look on his face was strange, wild, vain; I said,
What in the name of God is going on? He started to laugh.

I served up the meal. For starters, corn on the cob.
Within seconds he was spitting out the teeth of the rich.
He toyed with his spoon, then mine, then with the knives,
the forks.
He asked where was the wine. I poured with a shaking hand,
a fragrant, bone-dry white from Italy, then watched
as he picked up the glass, goblet, golden chalice, drank.

It was then that I started to scream. He sank to his knees.
After we'd both calmed down, I finished the wine
on my own, hearing him out. I made him sit
on the other side of the room and keep his hands to himself.
I locked the cat in the cellar. I moved the phone.
The toilet I didn't mind. I couldn't believe my ears:

how he'd had a wish. Look, we all have wishes; granted.
But who has wishes granted? Him. Do you know about gold?
It feeds no one; aurum, soft, untarnishable; slakes
no thirst. He tried to light a cigarette; I gazed, entranced,
as the blue flame played on its luteous stem. At least,
I said, you'll be able to give up smoking for good.

Separate beds. In fact, I put a chair against my door,
near petrified. He was below, turning the spare room
into the tomb of Tutankhamen. You see, we were passionate
then,
in those halycon days; unwrapping each other, rapidly,
like presents, fast food. But now I feared his honeyed embrace,
the kiss that would turn my lips to a work of art.
And who, when it comes to the crunch, can live
with a heart of gold? That night, I dreamt I bore

his child, its perfect ore limbs, its little tongue
like a precious latch, its amber eyes
holding their pupils like flies. My dream-milk
burned in my breasts. I woke to the streaming sun.

So he had to move out. We'd a caravan
in the wilds, in a glade of its own. I drove him up
under cover of dark. he sat in the back.
And then I came home, the woman who married the fool
who wished for gold. At first I visited, odd times,
parking the car a good way off, then walking.

You knew you were getting close. Golden trout
on the grass. One day, a hare hung from a larch,
a beautiful lemon mistake. And then his footprints,
glistening next to the river's path. He was thin,
delirious; hearing, he said, the music of Pan
from the woods. Listen. That was the last straw.

What gets me now is not the idiocy or greed
but lack of thought for me. Pure selfishness. I sold
the contents of the house and came down here.
I think of him in certain lights, dawn, late afternoon,
and once a bowl of apples stopped me dead. I miss most,
even now, his hands, his warm hands on my skin, his touch.

Carol Ann Duffy

I have used this poem with pupils as young as Year 9, but would usually save it for Year 10; it is ideal with sixth form. What makes this poem so convincing is the use of detail, and the language, 'its little tongue / like a precious latch', 'a hare... / a beautiful lemon mistake'. I also like the way Carol Ann Duffy simply ignores aspects of the story that do not interest her, for example that he was a king. The anachronisms are a source of humour and paradoxically make the poem more convincing, particularly the caravan, and the spare room looking like the tomb of Tutankhamen.

Mrs Midas comes from 'The World's Wife'; other poems in the sequence are Queen Kong, Mrs Aesop, Mrs Tiresias and Mrs Darwin. It is an excellent idea; the woman partners of famous men from the past, fact and fiction. You could ask students to write another in the sequence, Mrs Earp, Ms Canute. Alternatively, you could ask them to write from the point of view of the husbands of famous women, (whether or not they were married is of course irrelevant); Mr Boadicea, Mr Nightingale. Or simply write a monologue from the point of view of the famous person. If they do this, I suggest you get them to write about the character when they are not actually doing the thing for which they are famous, for example, Mussolini ironing his uniform, Cleopatra changing a fuse... This relieves them from the pressure of having to incorporate authentic detail.

LUCIFER'S MOTHER

He grew up such a good boy.
Blonde hair.
Blue eyes.
Angelic smile.
He never spoke out of turn.

I don't know where we went wrong.
He never smoked.
He took off his shoes on the mat
right until the end.

Then he changed.

Started wearing black
under his cape.
The feathers started dropping from his wings.
He painted his nails
until they stayed that colour anyway.

He moved out.
We don't speak now.

Catie Chapman (Year 9)

What I like about this is the understatement, the way Catie Chapman leaves so much unsaid, and leaves the detail to do the work, 'he took off his shoes on the mat / right until the end'. Also the casual mention of wings.

Drafting: how much help do you give them?

I am often asked how much I help students with their poems. The answer is that I make suggestions and leave the final decision to them. The aim is always to help young people to say what they want to say. This sounds simple but in fact it isn't; we often say what we think we ought to say, or we say too much. As in writing my own poems, it is a matter of identifying the poem within the draft and uncovering it. It's like Michelangelo, who apparently said that his sculptures involved uncovering the statue that is already in the stone. I made one suggestion to Catie Chapman, when she wrote 'Lucifer's Mother': try it without the last line. Originally, she had an extra line, which was 'of course'. And the poem doesn't need it. Of course.

Leave out the last line

The suggestion to leave out the last line or the last stanza is one of the most common pieces of advice that I give. This is particularly true if the student feels strongly about the subject they are writing about and wants to leave the reader in no doubt. I tell them that they need to credit the reader with intelligence, no one likes to be badgered. I also often suggest leaving out the first line, or the first stanza, if they have wasted time establishing setting when it isn't necessary, for example.

THINGS TO DO WITH A POEM

Things to do with a poem: sequencing

Cut up a poem that the class are unfamiliar with, give it to them and ask them to piece it back together, working in groups. The advantage of this is that it gets them to focus on the poem, it also provides instant motivation, an irresistible spirit of competition and ultimately the satisfaction of 'getting it right'. More importantly, it provides a lively context for the discussion of the finer points of a poem. It works particularly well with narrative poems such as 'Oh What is that Sound?' by W. H. Auden and would undoubtedly work with 'Mrs Midas'. The physical process of moving bits of a poem around and trying them out is certainly satisfying. Use it with all age groups, including sixth form. Once a class have worked on a poem in this way, arguing and justifying their choices, they are very intimate with it, so you could use it with a poem you are going to use for a piece of course work. The disadvantage of the exercise is that it treats the poem as a puzzle, with the teacher holding the right answer; not necessarily the best assumption to hold if we want to encourage open debate. Also, there is a lot to be said for giving the class the poem as it is meant to be read, and personally I wouldn't do it with certain poems, such as 'Mrs Midas' because it dilutes the impact that the poem has when it is first read. On the other hand, it's not going to do any harm if poems are used in other ways as well.

The CLOZE procedure (missing out every fourth word or so, and getting groups to work out what would fit, arguing for their best choice) is, like sequencing, a tried and tested procedure for developing reading skills. It is profoundly unsatisfying as a way into a poem, but it does alert students to diction, and it could be useful as a reminder for their own writing: that every word should count.

Sequencing: a creative approach

You can use sequencing with drafts of poems written by your students, if they are happy with the idea: cut up an early draft of a poem someone is working on, give it to different groups, and see how many alternative structures they can come up with. Playing around like this is an excellent way of coming up with new ideas and insights. The advantage here is that there is no right answer, so the discussion is more open-ended, constructive and genuinely useful. Of course this does not have to be done in groups; you could get everyone in the class to cut up their poems and experiment by trying out different structures. 'Sacrifice' by Taufiq Rafat has a fascinating structure, moving back and forth in time and switching points of view, and illustrates some of the possible advantages of abandoning conventional chronological structure and the effect that it can have. Sequencing, then, is a powerful tool for experimenting with poems.

Another productive and stimulating way into monologues is to liberate characters from fiction, and place them in unlikely settings:

TOM AND JERRY VISIT ENGLAND

O boy, I thought. A chance
to visit England and O boy here, out
of nowhere, a voice to describe it. Reader,
I dreamt of coming back to tell you how I marched
round the Tower of London, in a beefeater suit,
swished my axe at Jerry, belted after him
into the Bloody Tower, my back legs
circling like windmills in a gale
while ravens flapped around our heads.
You would hear it all: tea with the Queen
at Buckingham Palace and me scattering
the cucumber sandwiches at the sight
of Jerry by the silver salver. I couldn't wait
for the gorgeous tableau: Queenie with her mouth
in a little shocked screaming shape, her crown
gone crooked as she stood cringing on the throne
with her skirts up round her knees, and Jerry
down there laughing by the footstool.
I would be in a concertina zig-zag by that time
with a bone china cup stuffed in my face
and a floral tea pot shoved on my head so hard
my brains would form a spout and a handle
when it cracked and dropped off.

I can't get this new voice to explain to you
the ecstasy in the body when you fling
yourself into such mayhem, open yourself
to any shape at all and able to throw out
stars of pain for everyone to see.

But reader, the visit wasn't like that.
I ended up in a poem and it made me uneasy.
Cats prefer to skulk and sulk
in the dark, we prefer mystery
and slinking. This is even true of me

with my stupid human face opening
into only two or three stupid expressions:
cunning, surprise and maybe rage.
And I couldn't find Jerry.
'Where's the mouse?' I tripped
over commas and colons hard like diamonds, looking
for him. 'Where's the mouse?' I kept asking,
'Where's the mouse?' I banged full face into a query –
and ended up with my front shaped
like a question mark for hours. That was scary:
I usually pop right back into myself in seconds.
So I hesitated for once before flinging myself
down the bumpy staircase where all the lines ended.
I went on my rear and at the bottom you would have seen me,
end up, bristling with splinters, and nose down
snuffling for any trace of mouse smell.
Reader, it was my first tragic movie:
I couldn't find the mouse.

Jo Shapcott

Jo Shapcott writes:

In my poem, 'Tom and Jerry Visit England', the character who speaks is Tom, the cat from the cartoon show 'Tom and Jerry'. You'll remember he is almost completely silent in the cartoon, so it was great fun to dream up what he might say if he had the chance. In my poem he becomes a shape-changer, a protean character who, I think, in some ways stands for the figure of the poet. When I look at this poem with students, I often ask them to write their own poem in the voice of their favourite cartoon character. To make things more difficult and, always, more interesting, I ask them to put the character somewhere s/he wouldn't normally be, just as in my version he becomes trapped inside a poem. The resulting friction or frustration can lead to poems which dig down unexpectedly deep. I've seen surprisingly moving poems emerge from this idea starring, for example, Tweety Pie giving a press conference or Spiderman in the British Library.

The idea of giving a voice to a character who is normally silent is very potent. The first part of the poem is how Jerry imagines he would enjoy

London, the second is what happens in reality. Pupils could use a similar structure too: they could perhaps borrow Jo Shapcott's phrases; 'I dreamt of...' for the first part of the poem, and 'I ended up . . . ' for the second. A neat variation for the pupils on the structure of 'Ten Pence Story' in the previous chapter.

::THE LITTLE AWL THAT UNTIES KNOTS

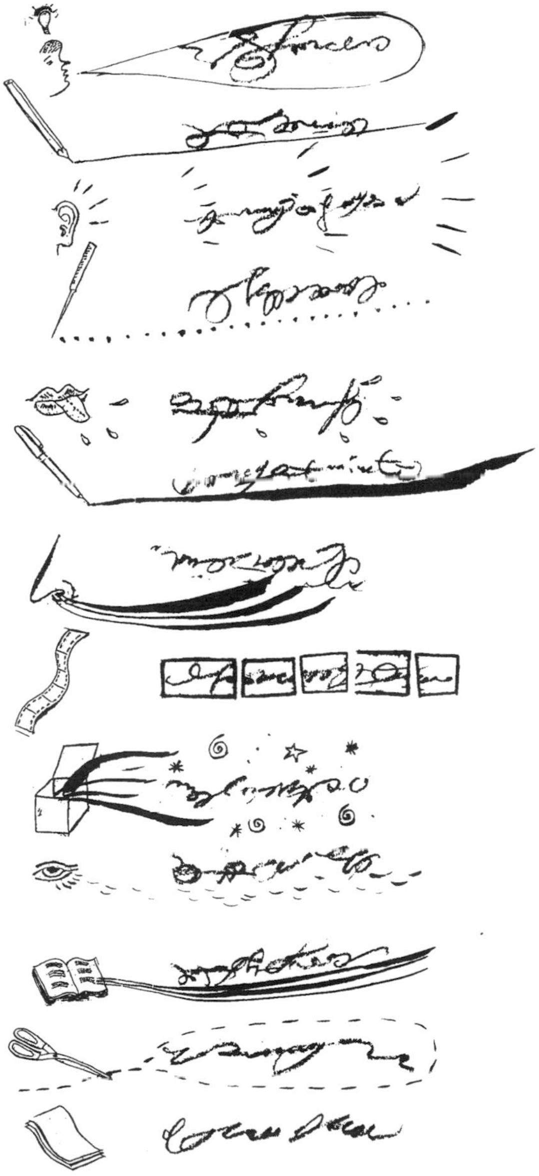

THE SONNET IS one of the most useful forms I have used in school; even if pupils do not manage to write one that satisfies them, the next time they write a poem they will write better for having had the experience of the longer line and the fourteen line structure. One sonnet that works particularly well in school is by Mick North. I bought his Littlewood book in a bookshop in Liverpool, attracted by the marvellous title, *The Pheasant Plucker's Son*, having first come across him in an interview published in the magazine, *Harry's Hand*. Mick North manages to make the tricky Shakespearean sonnet seem surprisingly effortless in this one about his father.

THE FINGER

You were always your shift's First-Aider:
St. John's Ambulance classes every year
to keep your hand in, Rescue Team member
(formed after the chimney fell), blood-donor –
hardly a day off sick yourself until
the hollow bone of your finger-end cracked
like a shell, caught between two barrels.
You couldn't believe it, flat on your back
with a finger! Hospital, operation –
amazed, you told us how they'd scrape a hip,
lift a bit for your digit and graft it on.
Which is how it's done Dad – you're put to sleep
and given back what's always been your own:
sick-pay and compensation, blood, flesh, bone.

Mick North

I really like the powerful combination of tenderness and controlled anger in 'The Finger', and the way Mick North uses the sonnet to accommodate a complex narrative structure. Also the way he uses the rhythms of speech while doing justice to the demanding form. When I read it with a class it takes a while for them notice that it rhymes. This is good for their own writing: it demonstrates how rhyme doesn't have to draw attention to itself, how you can embed it, make it all the more powerful by using enjambment and caesura to keep the poem moving past the end rhymes.

The poem also demonstrates how you can use internal rhyme; like the internal half-rhyme of 'compensation' with 'own' and 'bone', which consolidate the impact of the final couplet. It's that final couplet that makes the Shakespearean sonnet so tricky; it's hard to 'earn the punch line', and to stop it sounding too much like a punch line.

Mick North writes:

> 'The Finger' came about through a need to tell this story. What the need was I didn't recognise or acknowledge until later. The start was simply the memory of this incident coming to the surface of my mind, with 'raw material' stamped on it. Most of my poems have happened in this way – in retrospect I see more of the context, see more of what was going on around them.
>
> A few years before writing the poem I'd worked at the same factory as my father for two and a half years, doing similar work. At the time of writing it, I think I'd been reading a lot of James Kelman. There's a devastating, one-paragraph story of his in *Not Not While The Giro* called 'Acid' (about an industrial accident). I needed to express the anger you've noted, and likewise tenderness – but that's what I found in the making of the poem, not what I consciously started with. A need to get closer to my father and defend him in some way; defend or speak up for everybody who does this kind of work without anybody knowing the price.
>
> The department of 'our' factory he worked in made something called Transprint – huge rolls of thin paper printed with patterns which would then, somewhere else, be heat-transferred onto fabric for anything from curtains to dress material. And no-one hanging those curtains would know what a dirty hole their pretty pattern came from.
>
> So, 'The Finger' is a collage of politics and feelings and stuff I've read, glued together with personal and family history, mounted on or framed by the sonnet. It's poetry as a way of working things out in terms of self-discovery and your stance to the world; an aspiration to pick up Heaney's spade/pen for digging with; even better, Gary Snyder's 'a tool, a net or trap to catch and present; a sharp edge; a medicine, or the little awl that unties knots'.

Yes, but did the writer intend this?

When I read poems with a class, one of the questions that comes up time after time is, are we reading too much into this? Could someone really intend to pack this much meaning into so few words? I tell them that when you are writing well, you sometimes only really understand what you have written some time later, it's as if there is more of 'you' writing the poem than you are aware of. You surprise yourself. I also mention that when pupils show me a poem that they have written, I sometimes point out things that they have done that they did not intend, or maybe even notice; the use of half-rhyme, for example, subtly reinforcing a meaning. Another way of talking about this is to listen to writers talk about their work, as Mick North does here. My Year 11 class who had already read 'The Finger' were intrigued by Mick North's story of the poem, how it came about and what was in his mind when he wrote it.

Drafting: selected poems

The complexity of what goes into a poem like 'The Finger', highlights the demands we are making when we ask pupils to write poems for us. Even the time scale (completing a poem in one week, for example) is particularly rigorous, considering the ways in which many writers go about writing poems. What I do to try to accommodate contradictions like this is to encourage pupils to keep copies of their poems and sometimes to redraft them, much later, for a different purpose; for an anthology, for display, or for a competition. This encourages young people to see poems as constantly evolving and comes closer, I think, to the 'normal' process of writing poetry. You can take this further by asking the children to produce their own 'Selected Poems' towards the end of a school year.

Writing sonnets

When the class are writing sonnets, I am relaxed about whether they 'get it right' or not. The important thing is to write well, not to avoid being arrested by the poetry police. Sometimes a student will start writing a sonnet and the poem will turn into something else, it will be too long or short, or it will work better in lines of an uneven length. They will ask me if this is okay. The answer is always yes. The purpose is to write a good poem, not distort something into a sonnet that isn't. It's the same with iambic pentameter, or any other metre. In any case, it's more important, in my view, to get young people to write using the rhythms of their own speech. Having said that, a number of English teachers have told me how they manage to get children writing, and even speaking, in iambic pentameter... and there is always Tony Harrison.

You can use Mick North's 'The Finger' as a stimulus for pupils' poems by focusing on its content. Any group likes to tell the stories of their accidents. The sonnet form provides a structure in which to contain these narratives.

INDIGNATION OF A SEVEN-YEAR-OLD

Wooden tiles in the kitchen glow gently,
Forever zig-sagging away as we
Glide like ice-skaters, slipping and sliding,
Laughing and shrieking and crash landing,
Dusters and beeswax tied to our feet.
No way to stop as the black iron pot
Looms ahead, billowing smoke signals.
The boiling water hits my skis – gerbils
Stir in their graves, the dead roused by my screams.
Rushing to hospital with Mum in the back
100 mph, blisters and cream
And the nurse, smiling, joking,
Calling me a drip!!

Kate Lines (Year 10)

Kate Lines writes:

Before I wrote 'Indignation Of A Seven-Year-Old' we read at school 'Shall I compare thee to a summer's day?' by William Shakespeare and two other sonnets called 'The Finger' and 'Trio' by Mick North. Sonnets are meant to have about 10 syllables per line and I tried to make all my lines about that length. My poem also has bits of half-rhyme, but the rhyming pattern is a bit irregular. For the poem we had to write about something that happened to us, and I called it 'Indignation of a Seven-Year-Old' because I was really annoyed when the nurse called me a drip (I was really wet all over). I like the line 'no way to stop as the black iron pot' because 'stop' and 'pot' are a half-rhyme and I think they make the poem flow in a way, because that point in the story is meant to be quite hurried and rushed. I would have liked to get some of my rhymes a little better, because I would have liked to put more in at the end, but I didn't have time.

Commentaries

Students need to read their own poems as attentively as they read the poems of established writers. One way of encouraging this is to get them to write commentaries, occasionally, on the poems that they have written. This is standard procedure, of course, with poems written as course work for 'A' level English Language, though the aims are different. Commentaries need not be exhaustive; just a few key points, for example on how they came to write the poem and perhaps on how the poem changed between drafts. This encourages students to pay extra attention to editing. I have used commentaries with younger children, but nothing too detailed, the poem is the main thing. Another option is a verbal commentary; reading out their poems and talking about how they wrote them.

Making the familiar strange

Some contemporary sonnets play fast and loose with the form. I would read this next one with Year 10 and above, probably saving it for Year 12. I wouldn't read all these sonnets in one go, or necessarily during the same year with a particular class, I would come back to the sonnet by using a good example. One of the advantages of using poems as models is that the children need not necessarily realise that they are revisiting familiar territory. Furthermore, I wouldn't necessarily introduce a poem as a sonnet; I would read the poem first and probably wait for a member of the class to identify it as one. The most important thing is the poem itself, and this one is remarkable:

SWINEHERD

'When all this is over', said the swineherd,
'I mean to retire, where
Nobody will have heard about my special skills
And conversation is mainly about the weather.

I intend to learn how to make coffee, at least as well
As the Portuguese lay-sister in the kitchen
And polish the brass fenders every day.
I want to lie awake at night
Listening to cream crawling to the top of the jug

And the water lying soft in the cistern.

I want to see an orchard where the trees grow in straight lines
And the yellow fox finds shelter between the navy-blue trunks,
Where it gets dark early in summer
And the apple-blossom is allowed to wither on the bough’.

Eiléan Ní Chuilleanáin

I really like the way the poem begins, not wasting any words establishing context or setting. Eiléan Ní Chuilleanáin refers to a whole world in which the reader immediately believes, e.g. ‘the Portuguese lay-sister in the kitchen’, ‘the brass fenders’, ‘the navy-blue trunks’ of the trees.

She doesn’t bothering to explain, justify, or fill in the blanks, but allows the detail to stand up for itself: ‘Listening to cream crawling to the top of the jug / And the water lying soft in the cistern’. The poem invents a world and makes it believable. If Roger McGough in ‘First Day at School’ makes the familiar into something strange, this poem can be said to work the other way; to make the strange familiar.

Things to do with a poem: the imaginary commentary

I probably wouldn’t use ‘Swineherd’ as a model for students’ own writing because I suspect it would be too difficult; the poem is astonishingly ‘complete’. What I might do, though, is ask students to imagine that they wrote it, and then to write a commentary as if they were the author. They could say where they got the ideas from, how much of it is ‘true’ and how the poem changed between drafts. I don’t imagine that they would necessarily come up with anything remotely like a commentary that Eiléan Ní Chuilleanáin might be persuaded to write, and this is not the intention. The intention rather is to encourage students to look at the poem as a final draft, and to attempt to ‘trace it back’. In the process of doing this, they will be encouraged to begin to unravel some of the poem’s complexities and find ways into it. As an entertaining way into this exercise, tell them to imagine that the first impulse for the poem came from an experience as remote from the world of the poem as they can imagine. (Queuing for a bus in the rain, they overhear the conversation behind them..?)

Another contemporary sonnet that takes liberties with the form and gets away with it is this one, from the sequence 'Book of Matches' in the book with the same name, by Simon Armitage:

*

I am very bothered when I think
of the bad things I have done in my life.
Not least that time in the chemistry lab
when I held a pair of scissors by the blades
and played the handles
in the naked lilac flame of the bunsen burner;
then called your name, and handed them over.

O the unrivalled stench of branded skin
as you slipped your thumb and middle finger in,
then couldn't shake off the two burning rings. Marked,
the doctor said, for eternity.

Don't believe me, please, if I say
that was just my butterfingered way, at thirteen,
of asking you if you would marry me.

Simon Armitage

One of the hardest poems to write is the love poem and this one uses some of the ingredients; 'O the...', 'for eternity...', 'asking you if you would marry me'. At the same time, words like 'bunsen burner', 'butterfingered' and the 'chemistry lab' demonstrate how the sonnet can be made to accommodate the everyday and the mundane. The co-existence of the two registers in the poem reflects the confusion of the narrator which results in his disastrous attempt to attract the attention of the girl he admires. Technically, the poem is useful for students' writing because it demonstrates that a form doesn't have to be a straitjacket. The rhymes are irregular, they don't draw attention to themselves, and even the final rhyme, 'eternity' and 'marry me', with the half rhyme 'I say' between them, is entirely convincing without being distracting.

THINGS TO DO WITH A POEM

Things to do with a poem: borrow a line...

...and use it as the first line of a new poem. After reading the Simon Armitage poem with a Year 10 class, I have had very good confession-type responses from simply giving students the first line, 'I am very bothered when I think...' and asking them to write down what it suggests to them, to continue the poem, or simply 'free write'. In fact Simon Armitage explains how he borrowed the first two lines of this poem, 'I am very bothered when I think / of the bad things I have done in my life' from a character assessment questionnaire that he used when he worked for the probation service. So a line can be borrowed to start off a poem from any type of text, however unlikely.

A variation on this exercise is that when they have been writing for a few minutes, read out a new line, tell them to write that down too, and carry on from this point. The interruptions have the effect of encouraging pupils to explore new directions, unfamiliar territory. You can do the same thing with sentences from a novel; a favourite of mine for this purpose is *The Big Sleep* by Raymond Chandler. I flip through the book and take sentences more or less at random. Dialogue works particularly well. If someone is writing something they really like of course, it is okay for them to carry on writing and ignore your interruptions; as I said earlier, the aim of any writing exercise is not to impose restrictions for their own sake, but to encourage young people to write.

The opening line of many poems are invitations to further poems. Another poem that works particularly well in this context is Seamus Heaney's 'Early Purges', which begins, 'I was seven when I first saw kittens drown'. Give a class the structure of the line; 'I was... when I first...', tell them to fill in the gaps and continue. They could write about ordinary everyday things like riding a bike or swimming a length, or something more dramatic. I've had some arresting openings;, including one in dialect written from the point of view of a character from the novel *Trainspotting*; 'Ah remember when / Ah first tried smack / The contents of the spoon / Was heated over a candle // –Want me tae do it? / Mother Superior asked...' (Alice Brierley, Y11).

12::SOME WORDS OF ADVICE

IN THE LAST chapter I dealt with sonnets and how I go about using the form with young people. In this chapter I want to take the notion of form into another area, an area which can happily accommodate 'the fifteenth to twenty-first / lines in a sonnet'; the area of lists. Lists provide an accessible and fruitful way into writing poems. They can provide a form that has no formal restrictions, that is only limited by the number of things that the writer includes in their list. It is a kind of formless form.

One of the most powerful books I have ever read is Dee Brown's *Bury My Heart at Wounded Knee*, the history of the American West from the point of view of the Native American, culminating in the Wounded Knee massacre. How can you write a poem about something like that?

IT HAS COME TO THIS

The Chiefs:
Rain in the Face
Red Cloud
Long Dog
Charging Hawk
Young Man Afraid of His Horses
Crow Foot
Kicking Bear

In a museum, in a German city
I greet your photographs.
Your names give me a story
I can't write,
a story I can only dream
on warm nights.

Burial of the Dead
at the Battle of Wounded Knee S.D.
CopyRighted Jan. 1st 1891
by the North Western Photo Comp.
Chadron Neb. No. 1.

Who owns the dead? Who owns

the burial? What would you say
Sun in the Pupil
Red Shirt Girl
Has a Dog
Spotted Thunder
Cast Away and Run
Wounded in Winter
Shedding Bear
Shake the Bird
Bring Earth to Her?

Your names are stuck
in my mind – I want to keep
them: I want to imagine the eyes, teeth,
voices, fingers – that lived in your names.

Sujata Bhatt

The power of this poem is in the names, as Sujata Bhatt suggests. It is particularly evocative because these names were 'earned': they tell us about their owners' lives, stories of things that they did or that happened to them, stories that made them memorable.

A list can often be used as a basis for a poem. Many poems make use of lists. There are many possibilities, using lists, to record and remember, or for social comment and protest (or both, as with Sujata Bhatt's poem). Subjects could include the names of boats sunk during a particular war, the names of coalfields closed down at the time of the miners' strike, for example.

I once had to teach a GCSE History group who were studying British Social and Economic History. It was Thursday afternoon, a very hot, dozy day and we were looking at a map of British coalfields. The class's attention, and mine, was flagging. To rev up the proceedings I told them that when I said 'Go!' they had to sing the names of the coalfields. There were a couple of rules: they had to sing as loudly as they could (any tune they liked) and they had to stop when I raised my hand. I'm sure they still haven't forgotten the names of those coalfields. With a little more time I'd have had the class in groups, putting the list of coalfields into some kind of order and performing them as poems. But the bell went.

List poems can be purely entertaining. Ian McMillan once performed a poem on BBC Radio One's *Mark Radcliffe Show*, consisting entirely of the names of islands off the Scottish coast, and another using the names of characters in Biggles novels. Names are evocative, and we can use this in the classroom. Collect the names of streets in the locality, for example, and get a class to arrange them in such a way as to read them aloud as if they were sinister and menacing, or write the outline of the first episode of a soap opera, in the form of a short poem, using street names as if they were the names of characters.

The following poem makes use of a list and demonstrates the opportunity that a list gives for focusing on rhythm: arranging words for the way they sound. The poem appears to combine seemingly random details and events; you cannot predict what is coming next. But the rhythm gives it unity, and makes it unforgettable.

THE WAY WE LIVE

Pass the tambourine, let me bash out praises
to the Lord God of movement, to Absolute
non-friction, flight, and the scarey side:
death by avalanche, birth by failed contraception.
Of chicken tandoori and reggae, loud, from tenements,
commitment, driving fast and unswerving
friendship. Of tee-shirts on pulleys, giros and Bombay,
barmen, dreaming waitresses with many fake-gold
bangles. Of airports, impulse, and waking to uncertainty,
to strip-lights, motorways, or that pantheon –
the mountains. To overdrafts and grafting

and the fit slow pulse of wipers as you're
creeping over Rannoch, while the God of moorland
walks abroad with his entourage of freezing fog,
his bodyguard of snow.
Of endless gloaming in the North, of Asiatic swelter,
to laundrettes, anecdotes, passions and exhaustion,
Final Demands and dead men, the skeletal grip
of government. To misery and elation; mixed,

the sod and caprice of landlords.
To the way it fits, the way it is, the way it seems
to be: let me bash out praises – pass the tambourine.

Kathleen Jamie

This could be used as a model, writing a poem 'in praise of' something. Ask pupils to make a list of things, perhaps things that frighten and excite them, things that bore them, (the poem doesn't have to be about something they particularly like), or simply words that they like the sound of. Then combine them for the sound and rhythm, also using line breaks for rhythm and pace such as 'pulse of wipers as you're / creeping over Rannoch' and also for surprise and humour; 'driving fast and unswerving / friendship'.

They could also use the same circular structure, beginning and ending with the same words. This is a particularly satisfying structure; it has the value of removing the uncertainty of how to end the poem, before it is underway, thereby leaving the writer free to 'let rip' in the middle.

SOME WORDS OF ADVICE: AFTER HESIOD

Never believe the words you hear in popular songs.
Conversely, believe them all,
even the ones about changing the world and living forever.

If you habitually rise early and take a run around the park,
make sure that, on certain days, you sleep past noon.
(This advice is reversible.) Staying in bed all day
watching the snow fall with a pain in your belly
is not recommended, but a lot of soup is good,
and vigorous dreaming of architecture. If, nevertheless,
you have to worry, confine your worrying
to one subject: money is always a good choice.
Never worry about 'the absurdity of existence',
or similar large vaguenesses which are really like
the memory of a grandmother who died before you were born.
What good will it do you? And do not become enslaved to anything.

There are other more specific forms of advice. For example,

if you go to a party and the apartment in which it is being held
resembles a hotel lobby, or a fashionable gallery,
leave immediately. Also avoid at all cost
people who ask questions like: 'What kind of poetry
do you write?' or 'What's it like to live in Manchester?'

If you believe that God is good and drink innately evil,
do not try to convince your friends. You will find
that even in the most crowded social gatherings
a wide circle opens around you. You will be left
puzzling at the large abstract painting on the wall.

Music may surround you like an enormous blue and rose-streaked sky,
But, if you prefer Wagner to Mozart, you are probably in trouble.
A soul singer's voice may convince you that the future is a promise
that will be kept, but the average day is doubts
with a kind of half-assed, upbeat effect at the end.

But don't be disgusted.
It's time to get readjusted.

My Book of Evasive Moves
is published by *Apocrypha Press Ltd.*,
a wholly-owned subsidiary of
Inaction Universal
and you should read it today,
but I must ask you to wait for my epic novel
Discarded Lovers, which will contain
everything you need to know: it is at least
three volumes long, and unwritten.

John Ash

This poem also uses a list as a basis for its structure. John Ash's poems almost invariably go down well with young people, partly because they have rarely come across anything quite like them. Some lines of the poem are deliberately prosaic in tone, like the last stanza, yet he is also capable of arresting and unforgettable lines like, 'vigorous dreaming of architecture';

where he finds them, I don't know.

I successfully used this poem recently when I was invited to do a workshop in a sixth form college. I asked the group to write a list of lines giving advice as Ash does, including advice given to them by teachers, people at home and by their friends; playfully combining practical 'wisdom' with irrelevance as this poem does, deliberately surprising the reader.

Like John Ash, Les Murray, is so good that I'd feel guilty if my sixth formers left without reading him. Many of his poems have a celebratory quality (like the Kathleen Jamie poem. I thought I'd go for an up-beat last chapter!), a useful antidote to the kind of poems that this age group sometimes go for. I was just the same. Around that age I was heavily into Leonard Cohen.

THE QUALITY OF SPRAWL

Sprawl is the quality
of the man who cut down his Rolls-Royce
into a farm utility truck, and sprawl
is what the company lacked when it made repeated efforts
to buy the vehicle back and repair its image.

Sprawl is doing your farming by aeroplane, roughly,
or driving a hitchhiker that extra hundred miles home.
It is the rococo of being your own still centre.
it is never lighting cigars with ten-dollar notes:
that's idiot ostentation and murder of starving people.
Nor can it be bought with the ash of million-dollar deeds.

Sprawl lengthens the legs; it trains greyhounds on liver and beer.
Sprawl almost never says Why not? with palms comically raised
nor can it be dressed for, not even in running shoes worn
with mink and a nose ring. That is Society. That's Style.
Sprawl is more like the thirteenth banana in a dozen
or anyway the fourteenth.

Sprawl is Hank Stamper in *Never Give an Inch*
bisecting an obstructive official's desk with a chain saw.

Not harming the official. Sprawl is never brutal
though it's often intransigent. Sprawl is never Simon de Montfort
at a town-storming: Kill them all! God will know his own.
Knowing the man's name this was said to might be sprawl.

Sprawl occurs in art. The fifteenth to twenty-first
lines in a sonnet, for example. And in certain paintings;
I have sprawl enough to have forgotten which paintings.
Turner's glorious *Burning of the Houses of Parliament*
comes to mind, a doubling bannered triumph of sprawl –
except, he didn't fire them.

Sprawl gets up the nose of many kinds of people
(every kind that comes in kinds) whose futures don't include it.
Some decry it as criminal presumption, silken-robed Pope Alexander
dividing the new world between Spain and Portugal.
If he smiled *in petto* afterwards, perhaps the thing did have sprawl.

Sprawl is really classless, though. It's John Christopher Frederick Murray
asleep in his neighbours' best bed in spurs and oilskins
but not having thrown up:
sprawl is never Calum who, in the loud hallway of our house,
reinvented the Festoon. Rather
it's Beatrice Miles going twelve hundred miles in a taxi,
No Lewd Advances, No Hitting Animals, No Speeding,
on the proceeds of her two-bob-a-sonnet Shakespeare readings.
An image of my country. And would that it were more so.

No, sprawl is full-gloss murals on a council-house wall.
Sprawl leans on things. It is loose-limbed in its mind.
Reprimanded and dismissed
it listens with a grin and one boot up on the rail
of possibility. It may have to leave the Earth.
Being roughly Christian, it scratches the other cheek
and thinks it unlikely. Though people have been shot for sprawl.

Les Murray

This poem is also based on a kind of list: a list of Les Murray's deliberately personal definitions of 'sprawl.' Ask students to write their own poem on a different 'quality', as a similar kind of extended definition, using examples ranging indiscriminately from personal experience to events in History. Mick North suggests, for example, 'The Quality of Cool', starting each stanza with 'Cool is . . .'

'The Quality of Sprawl' is a great title, a neat combination of apparent opposites. Les Murray values 'sprawl' for its unpredictability, individuality and freedom from the restraints of convention. Sprawl, for me, is also the writing of poems and the teaching, not knowing precisely what is going to happen next and not minding. You go into the classroom and take it from there. The best lessons, like the best poems, are the ones where you surprise yourself. Someone asks something you didn't anticipate, it leads to something else and before you know it everyone is writing. Like a 'list poem', the only limitations are the ones we choose for ourselves.

Index of Poems

1::Henry's Clock

2::Jumpstarting the Poem

3::The Thrill of Writing

4::Making The Familiar Strange

5::Naming

6::The Eye of the Blackbird

7::Mushroomed

Index of Things To Do With A Poem

Bibliography

Poetry

Armitage, Simon, 'I am very bothered when I think' from *Book of Matches*, London: Faber and Faber, 1993

Armitage, Simon, 'Eighteen Plays on Golfing as a Watchword' from *Kid*, London: Faber and Faber, 1992

Armitage, Simon, 'Ten Pence Story' from *Zoom!* Newcastle-upon-Tyne: Bloodaxe Books, 1989

Ash, John, 'From Lorca's Letters' from *Disbelief*, Manchester: Carcanet, 1987

Ash, John, 'Some Words of Advice: After Hesiod' from *The Burnt Pages*, Manchester: Carcanet, 1991

Auden, W. H., 'Oh What is that Sound' from Collected Shorter Poems 1927-1957, London: Faber and Faber 1966

Basho, (trans. William J. Higginson) 'Old pond' from *The Haiku Handbook*, New York: Kodansha, 1985

Basho, (trans. X.J.Kennedy) 'In the old stone pool' from *An Introduction to Poetry* by X.J.Kennedy, London: Harper Collins, 1990

Basho, (trans. Lucien Stryck and Takashi Ikemoto) 'Old pond' from *The Penguin Book of Zen Poetry*, Harmondsworth: Penguin, 1981

Bhatt, Sujata, 'It Has Come To This' from *The Stinking Rose*, Manchester: Carcanet, 1995

Brautigan, Richard, 'Haiku Ambulance' from *The Pill Versus The Springhill Mine Disaster*, Boston MA: Houghton Mifflin/Seymour Lawrence, 1965

Buson, 'Such a moon' from *The Penguin Book of Zen Poetry*, Harmondsworth: Penguin, 1981

Buson, 'White lotus' from *The Penguin Book of Zen Poetry*, Harmondsworth: Penguin, 1981

Carver, Raymond, *A New Path to the Waterfall*, London: Collins Harvill, 1989

Chuilleanáin, Eiléan Ní, 'Swineherd' from *The Second Voyage*, Dublin: Gallery Press, 1977

Cook, Stanley, 'Photograph of Tennyson by Julia Cameron' from *Woods Beyond a Cornfield: Collected Poems*, Huddersfield: Smith/Doorstop, 1995

Constantine, David, 'Coltsfoot' from *Madder*, Newcastle-upon-Tyne: Bloodaxe Books, 1987

Constantine, David, 'Pillbox' from *A Brightness of Cast Shadows*, Newcastle-

upon-Tyne: Bloodaxe Books, 1980
Cope, Wendy, 'The Uncertainty of the Poet' from *Serious Concerns*, London: Faber and Faber, 1992
Duffy, Carol Ann, 'Mrs Midas' from *Selected Poems*, London: Penguin, 1994 and *The World's Wife* (forthcoming)
Duffy, Carol Ann, 'Stealing' from *Selling Manhattan*, London: Anvil, 1987
Farley, Paul, 'A Thousand Hours' from *The Boy from the Chemist is Here to See You*, London: Macmillan, Picador, 1998
Harmer, David and Martyn Wiley, 'Trainspotter' in *Against the Grain*, (ed. Ian McMillan), London: Thomas Nelson & Sons Ltd., 1989
Heaney, Seamus, 'The Early Purges' from Death of a Naturalist, London: Faber and Faber, 1966
Heaney, Seamus, 'Mid-Term Break' from *Death of a Naturalist*, London: Faber and Faber, 1966 and *Opened Ground: Poems 1966-1996*, London: Faber and Faber, 1998
Henri, Adrian, 'The New, Fast, Automatic Daffodils' from *Collected Poems* 1967-1985, Allison and Busby, 1986
Hughes, Ted, 'Thistles' from *Wodwo*, London: Faber and Faber, 1967
Jamie, Kathleen, 'The Way We Live' from *The Way We Live*, Newcastle-upon-Tyne: Bloodaxe, 1987
Lawrence, D. H., 'Bat' from *Birds, Beasts and Flowers, Collected Poems*, London: Jonathan Cape, 1923 and 1929
MacBeth, George, 'Owl' from *A Doomsday Book*, London: Scorpion, 1965 and *Collected Poems 1958-1982*, London: Hutchinson, 1989
McGough, Roger, 'First Day at School' from *In the Glassroom*, London: Jonathan Cape, 1976
McMillan, Ian, 'Sonny Boy Williamson is Trying to Cook a Rabbit in a Kettle' from *Dad, The Donkey's on Fire*, Manchester: Carcanet, 1994
Mitchell, Adrian, 'Icarus Schmicarus' from *Adrian Mitchell's Greatest Hits*, Newcastle-upon-Tyne: Bloodaxe Books, 1991
Mitchell, Adrian, 'Ten Ways to Avoid Lending Your Wheelbarrow to Anybody' from *Adrian Mitchell's Greatest Hits*, Newcastle-upon-Tyne: Bloodaxe Books, 1991
Morgan, Edwin, 'Hyena' from *From Glasgow to Saturn*, Manchester: Carcanet, 1973
Murray, Les, 'The Quality of Sprawl' from *The People's Otherworld*, Manchester: Carcanet, 1991

North, Mick, 'The Finger' from *The Pheasant Plucker's Son*, Todmorden: Littlewood, 1990
O'Hara, Frank, 'Les Etiquettes Jaunes' from *The Selected Poems of Frank O'Hara*, New York: Alfred A. Knopf, 1974
O'Sullivan, Maggie, 'Naming' from *In the House of the Shaman*, London: Reality Street, 1993
Plath, Sylvia, 'Mushrooms' from *The Colossus and other Poems*, London: Heinemann, 1957, Faber and Faber, 1967, and *Collected Poems*, London: Faber and Faber,
Popa, Vasko, 'The Little Box' from *Vasco Popa: Collected Poems* (trans. Anne Pennington), London: Anvil Press, 1997
Popa, Vasko, 'Winter', 'Snow', 'Head', 'Corpse' and 'Bearers', 'Needle', 'Trousers' from *The Golden Apple* (trans. Andrew Harvey and Anne Pennington) London: Anvil Press, 1980
Pound, Ezra, 'In a Station of the Metro' from *Personae*, New York: New Directions, 1926 and London: Faber and Faber, 1952
Rafat, Taufiq, 'Sacrifice' in the *NEAB Anthology* 1999 English/English Literature, London: Heinemann Education, '1999' from *Pieces of Eight: Eight Poets from Pakistan* (ed. Yunis Said), Oxford: Oxford University Press, 1971
Raworth, Tom, '8.06pm June 10th 1970' from *Moving*, London: Cape Goliard, 1971
Sansom, Peter, 'Bliss' from *January*, Manchester: Carcanet, 1994
Shapcott, Jo, 'My Life Asleep' from *My Life Asleep*, Oxford: OUP, 1998
Shapcott, Jo, 'Tom and Jerry Visit England' from *Phrase Book*, Oxford: OUP, 1992
Snyder, Gary, 'After weeks of watching the roof leak' from *The Back Country*, New York: New Directions, 1968
Stevens, Wallace, 'Thirteen Ways of Looking at a Blackbird' from *Collected Poems*, New York: Alfred A Knopf, 1954 and *Selected Poems*, London: Faber and Faber, 1953
Sweeney, Matthew, 'Johnjoe's Snowman' from *The Flying Spring Onion*, London: Faber and Faber, 1992
Taigi, 'In the melon patch' from *The Penguin Book of Zen Poetry* (trans. Lucien Stryck and Takshi Ikemoto) Harmondsworth: Penguin, 1977
Violi, Paul, 'Midnight Shift' from *Likewise*, New York: Hanging Loose Press, 1988

Williams, William Carlos, 'This is Just to Say' from *Collected Early Poetry*, New York: New Directions, 1938

Williams, William Carlos, 'To a Poor Old Woman' from *Collected Poems*, Manchester: Carcanet, 1968

Wright, Kit, 'The Magic Box' from *Cat Among the Pigeons*, London: Viking Kestrel, 1987

Yates, Cliff, 'Henry's Clock' from *Henry's Clock*, Huddersfield: Smith/Doorstop, 1999

Prose

Brownjohn, Sandy, *Does it have to Rhyme?* London: Hodder and Stoughton, 1980

Carey, Peter, *Bliss*, London: Faber and Faber, 1999

Chandler, Raymond, *The Big Sleep*, London: Hamish Hamilton, 1939

Chandler, Raymond, *The Long Goodbye*, London: Hamish Hamilton, 1953

Cheshire Poetry Pack, Cheshire Poetry Project 1988-94, Cheshire Education Authority, 1994

Forsyth, Bill, *Gregory's Girl: The Film Script*, Cambridge: Cambridge University Press, 1997

Hughes, Ted, *Poetry in the Making: An Anthology of Poems and Programmes from Listening and Writing*, London: Faber and Faber, 1967

Koch, Kenneth, *Rose, Where Did You Get That Red?* Teaching Great Poetry to Children, London: Random House, 1973

Koch, Kenneth and the Students of P.S.6 in New York City, *Wishes, Lies and Dreams: Teaching Children to Write Poetry*, New York: Chelsea House, 1970

Levertov, Denise, 'On the Function of the Line', *Chicago Review* (Black Mountain and Since - Special issue), reprinted in *The Stony Thursday Book No.8: American Odyssey* (ed. John Lilly)

McMillan, Ian (ed.), *Against the Grain*, London: Thomas Nelson & Sons Ltd., 1989

McMillan, Ian, 'Keep Talking' from *The Poetry Book for Primary Schools* (eds. Anthony Wilson with Sian Hughes) London: The Poetry Society, 1998

Miner, Earl, Ezra Pound: *The Japanese Tradition in British and American Poetry*, Princeton: Princeton University Press, 1958

Muldoon, Paul (ed), *The Faber Book of Beasts*, London: Faber and Faber, 1997

Roethke, Theodore, from 'Tedlock, The Legend and the Poet' (p.51) from *The Colour of Saying* (eds. Ralph N Maud and Aneirin Talfan Davies), London: Dent, 1963

Sansom, Peter, *Writing Poems*, Newcastle-upon-Tyne: Bloodaxe Books, 1994

Sweeney, Matthew and John Hartley Williams, *Writing Poetry and Getting Published*, London: Hodder and Stoughton, 1997

Acknowledgments

Thanks to the following people who provided original material for this book: Joe Broughton, David Constantine, Ian McMillan, Graham Mort, Mick North, Maggie O'Sullivan, Tom Raworth, Peter Sansom, Ann Sansom, Jo Shapcott, Nick Warburton, John Williams.

The author and publishers gratefully acknowledge permission to use copyright material in this book as follows.

Simon Armitage 'I am very bothered when I think' from *Book of Matches*, Faber and Faber, 1993; John Ash 'From Lorca's Letters' from *Disbelief*, Carcanet, 1987 and 'Some Words of Advice: After Hesiod' from *The Burnt Pages*, Carcanet, 1991; Basho 'Old pond'(trans. William J. Higginson) from *The Haiku Handbook*, Kodansha, 1985; Basho 'In the old stone pond' (trans. X.J.Kennedy) from *An Introduction to Poetry*, Harper Collins, 1990; Basho 'Old pond' (trans. Lucien Stryck and Takashi Ikemoto) from *The Penguin Book of Zen Poetry*, Penguin, 1981, copyright Allen Lane, 1977; Sujata Bhatt 'It has come to this' from *The Stinking Rose*, Carcanet, 1995; Richard Brautigan 'Haiku Ambulance' from *The Pill Versus the Springhill Mine Disaster*, Houghton Mifflin/Seymour Lawrence, 1965 by permission of Ianthe Brautigan Swensen; Buson 'White lotus' and 'Such a moon' (trans. Lucien Stryck and Takashi Ikemoto) from *The Penguin Book of Zen Poetry*, Penguin 1981, copyright Allen Lane, 1977; Eiléan Ní Chuilleánain 'Swineherd' from *The Second Voyage*, Gallery Press, 1977; Stanley Cook 'Photograph of Tennyson by Julia Cameron' from *Signs of Life*, Morton/Peterloo, 1972 and *Woods Beyond a Cornfield: Collected Poems*,

Smith/Doorstop 1995; David Constantine 'Coltsfoot' from *Madder*, Bloodaxe, 1987 and 'Pillbox' from *A Brightness of Cast Shadows*, Bloodaxe, 1980; Wendy Cope 'The Uncertainty of the Poet' from *Serious Concerns*, Faber and Faber, 1992; Carol Ann Duffy 'Mrs Midas' by permission of the author; Paul Farley 'A Thousand Hours' from *The Boy from the Chemist is Here to See You*, Macmillan, 1998; David Harmer and Martyn Wiley 'Trainspotter' by permission of David Harmer and Margaret Wiley; Seamus Heaney 'Mid-Term Break' from *New Selected Poems*, Faber and Faber, 19; Ted Hughes 'Thistles' from *Wodwo*, Faber and Faber, 1967; Kathleen Jamie 'The Way We Live'from *The Way We Live*, Bloodaxe, 1987; D.H.Lawrence 'Bat' from *The Complete Poems of D. H. Lawrence*, by permission of Lawrence Pollinger Limited and the Estate of Frieda Lawrence Ravagli; George MacBeth 'Owl' from *Collected Poems* 1958-1982, Hutchinson, 1989; Roger McGough 'First Day at School' from *In the Glassroom*, Random House, Jonathan Cape, 1976; Ian McMillan 'Sonny Boy Williamson is Trying to Cook a Rabbit in a Kettle' from *Dad, the Donkey's on Fire*, Carcanet, 1994; Edwin Morgan 'Hyena' from *From Glasgow to Saturn*, Carcanet, 1973; Les Murray 'The Quality of Sprawl' from *The People's Otherworld*, Carcanet, 1991; Mick North 'The Finger' from *The Pheasant Plucker's Son*, Littlewood Arc, 1990; Frank O'Hara 'Les Etiquettes Jaunes' from *The Collected Poems of Frank O'Hara*, Grove Press, 1974; Maggie O'Sullivan, 'Naming' from *In the House of the Shaman*, Reality Street Editions, 1993; Sylvia Plath 'Mushrooms' from *Collected Poems*, Faber and Faber, 1981; Vasko Popa 'The Little Box' from *Vasco Popa: Collected Poems* (trans. Anne Pennington), London: Anvil Press, 1997 and, 'Winter', 'Snow', 'Head', 'Corpse and Bearers', 'Needle', 'Trousers', from *The Golden Apple* (trans. Andrew Harvey and Anne Pennington) London: Anvil, 1980; Ezra Pound 'In a Station of the Metro' from *Personae*, New Directions, 1926 and Faber and Faber, 1952; Tom Raworth '8.06pm June 10th 1970' from *Moving*, Cape Goliard, 1971; Peter Sansom 'Bliss' from *January*, Carcanet, 1994; Jo Shapcott 'Tom and Jerry Visit England' from *Phrase Book*, Oxford University Press, 1992 and 'My Life Asleep' from *My Life Asleep*, Oxford University Press 1998, by permission of the author; Gary Snyder 'After Weeks of Watching the Roof Leak' from *The Back Country*, Copyright 1968, Gary Snyder. Reprinted by permission of New Directions Publishing Corporation; Wallace Stevens 'Thirteen Ways of Looking at a Blackbird' from *Selected Poems*, Faber and Faber, 1953;

Matthew Sweeney 'Johnjoe's Snowman' from *The Flying Spring Onion*, Faber and Faber, 1992; Taigi 'In the melon patch' (trans. Lucien Stryck and Takashi Ikemoto) from *The Penguin Book of Zen Poetry*, Penguin, 1981, copyright Allen Lane, 1977; Paul Violi 'Midnight Shift' from *Likewise*, Hanging Loose Press, 1988; William Carlos Williams 'This is Just to Say' from *Collected Early Poems*, Carcanet, 1968, and 'To a Poor Old Woman' from *Collected Poems*, Carcanet, 1968; Kit Wright 'The Magic Box' from *Cat Amongst the Pigeons*, Viking Kestrel, 1987; Cliff Yates 'Henry's Clock' from *Henry's Clock*, Smith/Doorstop, 1999.

Every effort has been made to contact copyright holders and to obtain permissions prior to publication. Should any omissions remain, the publishers welcome correspondence from those concerned.

Students' poems

Joe Broughton, 'Swarby': winner of the Chester and Ellesmere Port District poetry competition, 1988-89, published in *Cracks in the Pavement*, Upton-by-Chester County High School Anthology, 1989; Penny Buswell, 'Writing a Poem': winner in the Simon Elvin Young National Poetry Competition, 1998; Clare Carline, 'Parrot Plumes': winner of Chester and Ellesmere Port District Poetry Competition 1988-89, published in *Cracks in the Pavement*, Upton-by-Chester County High School Anthology, 1989; Catie Chapman, 'Lucifer's Mother': winner of Skelmersdale and Up Holland Young Writer's '98 Competition, runner-up in the Simon Elvin Young National Poetry Competition, 1998; Ben Cross, 'An Invasion': runner up in W. H. Smith Inky Foot competition, 1998, first publication *Inky Foot Anthology*, Macmillan, 1999, copyright W. H. Smith; Rachel Head, 'Outline of a Viking Ship (AD 1100)': published in *Cracks in the Pavement*, Upton-by-Chester High School Anthology 1989; Ruth Hite, 'Love Ballad To A Scott Boulder Mountain Bike, 16in frame, In Metallic Grey/Silver £625 ONO': first published in the *Times Educational Supplement* 'Young Poet of the Week'; Alexandra Hopkins, 'Animals Never Forget': winner BBC Poetry of War competition, 1989, published in *The Poetry of Protest* (ed. Simon Fuller) BBC/Longman, 1991; Katie, 'Electric Cowboy': Cheshire Poetry Pack, Cheshire Poetry Project, 1988-94, Cheshire Education Authority; William Kerley, 'James Bond': first published in the *Times Educational Supplement* 'Young Poet of the Week'; Jamie Scott, 'We Have Come For Your Lettuce': runner up in the Simon Elvin Young National Poetry Competition 1998; Virgil Scott, '6 Things Not To Be Done At The Cinema': runner-up in the Simon Elvin Young National Poetry Competition 1998; Luke Yates, 'Dehydrated in the English Room': winner in the Simon Elvin Young National Poetry Competition 1998, first published in the *Times Educational Supplement* 'Young Poet of the Week', winner in the W. H. Smith Young Writers Inky Foot competition, 1998, *Inky Foot Anthology*, Macmillan 1999, copyright W. H. Smith; Ruth Yates, 'Donkey': winner W. H. Smith Young Writers Inky Foot competition 1998, *Inky Foot Anthology*, Macmillan 1999, copyright W. H. Smith, winner Simon Elvin Young National Poetry Competition, 1998; Thomas Yates, 'Stork': first published in the *Times Educational Supplement* 'Young Poet of the Week' 1995.